Achiever's Trail – The Beginning

SORENS RUGHOOPUTH

authorHOUSE

AuthorHouse™
1663 Liberty Drive
Bloomington, IN 47403
www.authorhouse.com
Phone: 1 (800) 839-8640

Published by AuthorHouse 03/09/2020

ISBN: 978-1-7283-4493-5 (sc)
ISBN: 978-1-7283-4492-8 (hc)
ISBN: 978-1-7283-4491-1 (e)

Library of Congress Control Number: 2020901156

Print information available on the last page.

Any people depicted in stock imagery provided by Getty Images are models, and such images are being used for illustrative purposes only.
Certain stock imagery © Getty Images.

This book is printed on acid-free paper.

Because of the dynamic nature of the Internet, any web addresses or links contained in this book may have changed since publication and may no longer be valid. The views expressed in this work are solely those of the author and do not necessarily reflect the views of the publisher, and the publisher hereby disclaims any responsibility for them.

CONTENTS

ABOUT THE BOOK

Achiever's Trail is a book with a good autobiographical and inspirational blend. In simple language using very down-to-earth examples of events that can happen in anyone's life! Sorens Rughooputh gives practical and encouraging guidelines to all those struggling in our stressful world today, and explains how to be self-confident and move out from our comfort zone to attain success. His book is interesting and thought-provoking with some heart-wrenching situations when he narrates his childhood as a poor village boy, his relationship with his parents, siblings, neighbors and the death of his father. It is also moving to read when later in his work life he faces much distress, also impacting his family, and how he copes with the situation. He never gave up and by applying the Success Principles he kept moving on despite the odds.

His life purpose: Read-Learn-Share can be implemented by everyone to be a "better version of ourselves" as he says. Sorens explains clearly how to achieve our goals even we have a price to pay. Throughout the book, he makes good use of inspiring quotes from famous people. After reading it, you feel motivated and ready to go out and conquer the world!

I have read some motivational books by well-known authors, but reading a fellow countryman's first book, a great attempt I would reckon, gave me a sense of pride and went straight to the heart. I can only wish good continuation & success to Sorens and that he keeps on helping others by sharing his Achiever's Trail.

Rubina Salehmohamed – Professional Editor

ABOUT THE AUTHOR

One of four siblings from a poor family, born and brought up in Palma on the tiny island of Mauritius in the Indian Ocean, Sorens Rughooputh soared in life through toil, sacrifices and determination. He didn't have an easy childhood as a village boy helping his parents to meet both ends by raising a cow and selling the milk.

At a young age as soon as he stepped out of secondary school (by the way, Sorens disliked studies then!), though he had the opportunity to enroll at a university, he started working to help his parents financially. He obtained a job in an insurance company as underwriting officer in 1990 and moved on to another one in 1996, quickly demonstrating exceptional capabilities and he was appointed as Underwriter. His talent was acknowledged by an important conglomerate in 2000, the British American Insurance Company in Mauritius. Sorens, with his great potential and determination quickly climbed the career ladder to Project Manager – New Life Operations System, Operations Manager, Vice President – Technical Services, Senior Vice President – Business and Channel Development. Having successfully led teams of over 750 people, Sorens was selected in 2010 as finalist for Sales Director of the Year in the British Excellence Sales and Marketing Award (BESMA). 2012 brought a turning point in his life when he was seconded to Bramer Life - Botswana as Deputy CEO/Principal Officer until June 2015.

Sorens was a speaker at the first Pan-African Bancassurance & Alternative Distribution Channels Conference 2018 in Accra, on the topic "Embracing Disruption to meet Customer Expectations from Protection to Enrichment".   He holds an Executive MBA, Diploma in Insurance from the Chartered Insurance Institute UK, Fellow Certified Insurance Professional of the Australian and New Zealand Institute of Insurance and Finance (ANZIIF), a Fellow Member of the Institute of Sales and Marketing Management UK.   Currently, Sorens is the Chief Technical Officer at National Insurance Company in charge of the Life Insurance Operations.

While working, he also studied through distance-learning programs. In 2017, Sorens travelled to the US to become a Certified Canfield Trainer on The Success Principles; he has already introduced these principles to 450+ persons in his Achiever's Trail Workshops to develop and guide the upcoming leaders to live their dreams. He is also a Certified Trainer for Happy For No Reason by Marci Shimoff.

After a fruitful professional career, he has been working on his life purpose: READ, LEARN and SHARE with the aim to create a pathway to move forward and help people by imparting his knowledge. Achievers Trail is just the beginning.

Sorens is married to Shandya and they have an eighteen year old son. He enjoys traveling, reading books and the Internet and spending time with his family.

ACKNOWLEDGEMENTS

First of all, I would like to thank my wife Shandya and son Jihan, whom I love very much and who are always at my sides to help, support and encourage me in moving forward in every project I undertake. Writing this book was one of these projects and without their support it would never have seen the light of day. They are really the rubber bands that have catapulted me where I am today.

My mother, late father, and my in-laws: By sharing their life experience, they have helped me enjoy life differently. My editors, who have been important resources in helping me put the entire puzzle together. Their trust, friendship and commitment to excellence were reflected from our first meeting through the final edits of this book.

Deep appreciation to my mastermind partners Ruggerro, Michael and Sandar for pushing me every week to move forward and all those colleagues and friends who came in my life to transform me to what I have become in developing my Achiever's Trail.

Last but not least to all the authors of the hundreds of books I read, for sharing their experiences and helping us to be better versions of ourselves.

FOREWORD

By Marci Shimoff

What if you had the power to consistently transform your toughest challenges into golden opportunities?

We all know that life is a trail lined with good experiences as well as challenges. While the good experiences are always welcome, the challenges can be a bit more difficult to embrace. In his first book, *Achievers Trail – The Beginning*, Sorens Rughooputh lights a pathway for doing exactly that.

I first met Sorens when he joined my Happy For No Reason Certified Trainer Program in 2018. It was then that Sorens told me about his dream to write a book. I quickly learned that we had a friend and mentor in common, Jack Canfield. Sorens had recently become a Certified Canfield Trainer for *The Success Principles.*, the first one of his kind in his home country of Mauritius. I distinctly remember how he referred to one of Jack's Success Principles – *Ask! Ask! Ask!* when he asked me to write his foreword. In him, I recognized a kindred spirit. Sorens has not gone through life but rather grown through life and is dedicated to helping others by sharing what he's learned himself.

Achievers Trail – The Beginning is based on Sorens' experiences — where he started, his struggles and how he was able to get where he is today. His engaging and personal story speaks to the challenges we all face on our path to learn and grow as human beings. Emphasizing the importance of perspective, Sorens shows us just how powerful the lens of positivity can be in seeing the sweetness that life has to offer, even in our challenges.

From my 35 years of teaching and speaking, I believe that life is always giving us the opportunity to grow and expand our capacity to learn through our experience, good or bad. If I never struggled with unhappiness early on, I wouldn't have been inspired to create my work around happiness, which has given me so much meaning and purpose.

As you will discover in this very personal story, Sorens allows us to see that it's possible to create happiness not just despite your challenges, but because of them.

Endorsement

Achievers Trail – The Beginning is an engaging and practical guide that can truly transform your life journey. – Marci Shimoff – #1 NY Times bestselling author, Happy for No Reason and Chicken Soup for the Woman's Soul

INTRODUCTION

I meditated for quite some time before committing to writing this book. A few questions haunted me. Who would be interested in my story? And why? What added value would it bring to people's lives? I remembered browsing through social media and coming across a post that said, "Everyone has a story, and everyone should write a book to share their story." It captured my attention. I finally decided to get behind the desk and start writing. It helped me discover my life's purpose: to read, learn, and share.

So, why not share my own story, where I came from, and what I have become in the process? Yes, many people may have similar journeys. The difference is that I want to share an opportunity with people who are prepared to move forward in life and change their environments against all odds. My objective is to demonstrate how you can transform "impossible" to "I'M POSSIBLE."

Before holding the pen, I must admit that I had to muster up a lot of courage. I still remember what my mentor Brian Tracy shared—the Brian Tracy 4 Ds for achieving your goal: Desire, Decision, Discipline, and Determination. I knew it would be difficult, but I believed if I followed Brian's advice, I could do it.

The books *The Success Principles, The Law of Attraction* and most recently, *Happy for No Reason,* have been very helpful in motivating me to take on this journey. I noticed that every time I took a step forward, I was either moving toward my goals or away from them. Once I realized this, I decided to start interrogating my actions before taking them: would doing this bring me closer to my goal? If the answer is yes, I do it. If it's no, I don't.

After writing this book, I came to understand that the Almighty put me in a difficult situation so that I could grow. Good luck or bad luck, I managed to cope with these struggles. Looking back, I see that life is full of challenges. It's how you react to those challenges that will determine your future. I decided to take positive action and fought against all these struggles, and I went from riding a bicycle to owning my own brand new car. I am not saying this to brag about my achievement, but instead to prevent others from committing the same mistakes I made.

The comfort zone by The Wealth Hike (TWH) is a good demonstration of where one stands. [1]

The Comfort Zone	– Feeling safe and in control.
Fear Zone	– Lack of self-confidence, finding excuses, being attacked by others' opinions.
Learning Zone	– Dealing with challenges and problems, acquiring new skills.
Growth Zone	– Finding a purpose, living your dream, setting new goals, and conquering objectives.

I recalled the day I moved from the Fear Zone to the Learning Zone. My life started to change from the inside out. As many people have said, be ready to be comfortable being uncomfortable. It was not an easy task, but believe me, the result is wonderful.

My son Jihan introduced me to the film *The Boy Who Harnessed the Wind*. It's about a 13-year-old boy, William Kamkwanda, who is thrown out of the school he loves when his family can no longer afford the fees. He still sneaks into the library in order to learn how to build a windmill and save his village from a famine. As Dr. Myles Munroe said, "Your value attracts wealth." William manages to repurpose items he finds in

---

[1] https://www.the weathhike.com

the scrap yard. Because he worked hard teaching himself in the library and scouring for materials, he is able to build a windmill that saves his village. This inspiring adventure has motivated many people to remain positive against all odds. The day you find a chair in a tree, you are ready to change the world.

Embracing a new culture during my stay in Botswana, far from my family, helped me develop my own effulgence. I learned to understand how people stay happy and motivated despite tough situations. Some have no water, no electricity and yet they are still smiling. I have travelled to Delhi, Jaipur, Brazil, South Africa, Ghana, Nigeria, Zimbabwe, Malaysia, London, Paris, Amsterdam, Italy, United States and most recently Canada. All of these places have been inspiring and helped me find new facets of myself.

My profession as an underwriter, assessing and approving death and disability claims (not an easy task, I must admit) has helped me appreciate life and God's blessings to see a new sunrise. After spending almost 30 years in this industry, I have observed a change in the death and disability age profile. When I started my career, most of the claims were from people over the age of 60. Recently, this has changed, with most claims coming from the age group 35 to 45 for all sorts of diseases. Why I am telling you this? I want you to understand that time is ticking for all of us. Everyone has dreams. I don't know how many people fulfill their respective dreams or share their aspirations with others. How many have departed, taking along their secrets to the tomb?

So even if your story is one-pager, write it, and share it with others so that we can learn from it. Learning is key in all stages of life, from school to adulthood. Life experiences are always helpful. Aim higher spiritually, not materially. I am not relating to religion but instead to knowing oneself. As Jim Rohn rightly said, "Sight is when you see with your eyes and insight when you see with your mind." Pay attention to every single and subtle hint. Work out a game plan and take action to make your dreams come true. Whatever you are learning, turn that knowledge into substantial action.

We all have the capacity to be the leaders of our own lives, but some of us, decided to be followers. Your future intention determines your present action. Don't rely only on experience and luck. Knowledge, skills, and massive action will provoke the shift from the standard route to the fast lane. Remember, followers live the dreams of others. Leaders live their own dreams.

From Humble Beginnings

Now was I in a strait, and did not see
Which was the best thing to be done by me:
At last I thought, Since you are thus divided,
I print it will, and so the case decided.
-*The Pilgrim's Progress*

CHAPTER 1

Believe to Achieve

"Take the first step in faith. You don't have to see the whole staircase. Just take the first step." – Martin Luther King Jr.

Allow me to start by saying the following as formally as I can: My friends, always believe in yourself. Never lose hope and keep on believing in what you do. Remember, what you do now will have a domino effect in your life. Think and act wisely and you will achieve greatly.

I can still remember everything as if it happened yesterday: the taste of fresh cow milk, the smell of wet soil, green grasses, cow dung, sugarcane leaves, and cane juice oozing from crushed cane on the road. The beautiful scenery that Mother Nature gifted us was simply breathtaking.

The scene makes my heart pound at an extraordinary pace. This was home. These memories linger in my mind and shall remain there as long as I live. Mixed feelings of pride, sadness, and happiness dwell in my consciousness when I sit down to narrate this part of my story to my son or close friends. This is the beginning of my path, where it all started.

I call it the "Triggering Factor." The journey from where I began to where I am is a case study in the power of belief. Simply stated, I learned that one must believe to achieve. Believe in yourself and the achievement will follow.

Today, I am proud of where I stand. Tears roll down my cheeks when I remember myself as a kid trying to build my own car from metal scraps that I found in the fields. I was a big fan of cars and they became one of my passions. I recall having some plastic toy cars and trucks as a child. I took great care of them and felt proud as their owner. I displayed them on my wardrobe. They were my treasures, and I played with them every day.

Growing up in Palma

First things first, let me tell you about myself. I was born and raised in Quatre-Bornes, in Palma. Both are in Mauritius, a small African island nation in the Indian Ocean, east of Madagascar. The place is mesmerizing. You can feel time fly by as steadily as waves washing up the island's beaches. Life was not a bed of roses at that time, but it was full of magic.

Situated at around 1.5 km from the closest town, Palma was surrounded by sugarcane fields. At harvest time, they were covered with beautiful sugarcane flowers. It always looked like a huge green carpet to me. Dogs and chickens wandered around in the fields, feeding on whatever they could find.

On a few occasions, when the dogs got hungry, they did not hesitate to hunt the chickens, which ran helter-skelter for their lives. On street corners, children played happily; some skipping rope while others played hide and seek, "la marelle," the French name for hopscotch, or "sapsiwaye," a local child's game, originating from China, with no apparent English translation.

Many large trucks carrying stacks of sugarcane travelled the roads, cruising slowly towards the factory. As they approached via the main road, I appreciated and admired the orderly single file line they formed, a kind of "à la queue leu leu" (French for "single file").

I always respected the laborers on the roads, those who worked hard to clear the dry leaves from the streets' borders. They were and continue to be my role models, for living with discipline and courtesy. They woke up early in the morning every day and traveled to work. They ate lunch (curry with paratha, unleavened flatbread) under the shade of a tree. After they finished their simple meal, they went back to work.

I come from a family of very limited means: two elder sisters, a younger brother, my mother, my father and myself. Despite being poor in money, we considered ourselves wealthy in moral values, ethics, and our way of life. Although things were difficult and challenging for us, we managed to thrive day by day.

When sugarcane harvesting was over, the locality faced a kind of metamorphosis. Other types of vehicles and lorries arrived to load and unload rocks that were carried from the fields to the nearest stone-crushing mills.

I clearly recall the recklessness and high-speed driving of the lorries on our narrow roads. I even witnessed some accidents, which made me afraid of lorries. The bright side of this was that it made me tough and aware of how to deal with traumatizing situations from a tender age.

My Father

My father was a hard worker. However, he was an above standard alcoholic drinker. This is one circumstance that hurts me even now, after his passing. The circumstances of his life seemed to predetermine his alcoholism. He was a laborer working to sustain our family, but we could barely make ends meet. No matter how bad I felt about his drinking too much, I never lost my respect for him.

At a young age, my father and his elder brother lost their mother and their father remarried. From this new union came other half-brothers and half-sisters.

My father and his brother had to shoulder the responsibilities of the younger brothers and sisters. They bore all the whims of their stepmom and endured all the hardship that came from seeing to her demands.

One of his brothers, in an act of desperation, committed suicide since the family did not approve of his relationship with the girl he loved. She was from another religion. My father bore that weight for the rest of his life.

On the positive side, my dad was a talented artist, musician and accomplished dancer. Thanks to his talents, he was popular with the ladies especially those who were soon to be married as he could be relied upon to live up the party. Often, my father opened the dance floor with the new bride. It was a beautiful wedding spectacle, but not for my mother, who started feeling jealous. This led to some clashes between my parents. My father was always in a setting where alcohol and cigarettes were accessible. His alcohol consumption became excessive and he became addicted to it.

I strongly believe that in alcohol, he found an escape from life's harsh reality. A lack of guidance and awareness made it nearly impossible for my father to quit his drinking habit. We had no one who could intervene to stop him. I was still young, and I had no voice to ask him to change.

An alcoholic dad was the triggering factor to a lot of gossip amongst the neighborhood and family. Whenever I walked by, people would say, "This little guy got loads of liquor flowing in his veins. No doubt, he will surely end up like his dad." I tried to ignore them, but comments like these cut deep.

I used to go to the bar and wait for my dad, determined to get him back home safely. I did this all the time. "If I had a son like yours, I would have definitely killed him," said one of my dad's friends at the bar.

He considered me a leech who wouldn't let my dad have fun at the bar. But he didn't understand—I loved my dad and needed him to get home in one piece. I didn't want him to fall by the wayside or get into an accident on his way home, drunk.

My Mother

Abraham Lincoln stated, "All that I am, or hope to be, I owe to my angel mother." I love my mother for she is my everything. She doted on me with her love, comfort, time, and soul. She sacrificed so much to make my siblings and myself happy.

It was very difficult for my father to earn enough to sustain our family. My mother, my hero, decided to join forces to help contribute to our family income. Unfortunately, since my mother was not academically gifted, it was not easy for her to obtain a job. In fact, at that time, it was quite impossible for an uneducated woman to be employed.

My mother did not give up. She was offered a cow by her parents to raise and milk. She could sell the milk for additional income. I was told that, at that time, women in the same situation as my mother would often receive a cow from their parents as a gift or heritage. This would help them to have some cash inflows and make ends meet for their families.

Raising a cow meant having to feed it and take care of it. It provided for us, so we had to provide for it. Green grasses were its staple food at that time. I often accompanied my mother to cut grasses for the cow. It felt like an amazing adventure any kid would love to live.

I spent my school holidays in my mother's company at the foot of the mountain and in the fields. My mother made sure to inculcate me with moral values while we were cutting grasses. We developed a very close bond. I shared my secrets and my fears with her. She encouraged me and told me never to be sad in life no matter how things may turn up. My mom motivated me and always knew how to make me feel happy.

Even though I had to make several trips from our house to the mountains, I never grew tired. Instead, I felt proud as I was contributing to the chores and helping my parents. Moreover, I was always the "sales manager" for the milk we got from our cow. I had to canvass customers to come and buy our fresh milk.

More customers meant more income for my family. We also had to face some competition as there were other families who were also in the same milk-selling activity. I believe that this is where my passion for sales and bargaining originated. The persuasion and doggedness I practiced, as well as the virtues of tenacity and patience that I learnt, helped me excel in my business as an adult. This happiness and satisfaction I derived were among the best feelings a young eight-year-old boy could ever feel.

Lessons Learned

Have faith and allow the Lord to handle the rest. Sometimes we complain about our families, but we must have trust and faith that everything will work out.

Maybe your early childhood was like mine: a scene of poverty and embarrassment from the outside. But at the same time, it was adventurous and full of role models of kindness, creativity, and strength.

The love of my parents made up for the lack of money. Most of all, I established a belief that proved to be unshakeable even amid devastating odds.

That simple belief, born out of a childhood of challenge and innocence, is to always believe in yourself and never lose hope. Keep on believing in what you do.

CHAPTER 2

Endure the Struggle

"Everything you want is just outside your comfort zone." – Robert Allen

Like many children, I had big dreams. The sweet part is, I achieved them. I am proud to say that I made it. It would not have been possible if I had not worked hard, against all odds.

There were moments in my life when I was discouraged and searched for hope. Fortunately, I had parents by my side who cheered me up and taught me basic life lessons and moral values. "My son," they would say, "keep on believing in your dreams and never let go. You will become someone successful one day. Always stay humble and always remember your roots. Be always grateful to the Almighty. Never belittle people. Instead, help people in any way you can." These sacred words still resound in my ears. I shall always cherish my parents' lessons.

My Siblings

My siblings and I were alone most mornings. My sisters played the motherhood role when my mother was gone, working or running errands. They instinctively took the responsibility to look after me and my little brother.

Witnessing my elder sisters' efforts made me extremely proud of them. Together, we built characters defined by discipline, love, and care that positively impact our life today.

I remember being highly protective of my elder sisters. I presume that all brothers are. In my hometown, jobless guys were known to wander the streets, sometimes being disrespectful to the women they encountered.

One day, when my sisters accompanied my mother and I to cut grasses, a couple guys kept staring at my sisters and teasing them. Despite being only eight years old, I decided to take some action. What I did was simple, yet it carried complex consequences that I had to accept.

I approached my mother with a proposal. "Mother, please let my sisters remain at home while only the two of us go and cut the grasses since my little brother is too young. I do not want my sisters to be tired."

My mother's response was unprecedented. "My son, I shall agree to your request, but I have one condition."

"Tell me, Mom. What is your one condition?" I asked.

"While your sisters and little brother remain at home, you will have to do part of their job. You will need to cut more grasses and carry even more. Are you agreeable?"

Without thinking twice about it, I immediately answered "Yes!" From that day, as agreed, I took courage in both hands and cut even more grasses to prove to my mother that she made the right choice to trust me.

No matter what happens, never let the fear of failing prevent you from doing what's right. If you see something that you think you can do; do it. You might fail, but it will be better that you tried and failed than to have never attempted at all.

Young Life

I really did not like going to school. I wanted to drop out and start a course in car mechanics. But my parents and cousins encouraged and motivated me to stay in school.

Because I was a slow learner, I used to go and stay with my cousins Ramesh and Sanjay, who helped with my Mathematics lesson. I also loved staying with them because I got the chance to eat delicious meals prepared by my aunt. Her food might have been the source of my enduring love for Mathematics.

Most of the time, I borrowed my father's bicycle to head off on adventures in the fields or the nearby watercress plantation. I remember that with the help of a piece of cloth, I was able to catch a lot of fresh baby shrimps in a neighboring stream. We then cooked them for ourselves. Sometimes, I would give some to the neighbors. I also kept some in a bottle of water to watch them swim. Sadly, after some days, the shrimps died. I was naïve and did not know that they needed air.

It is sad to witness the changed scene today. With the infrastructure development in terms of roads, pavements, bridges, and buildings, these streams have been covered and no longer exist. Today, it is difficult to find any shrimp to catch. The insecticides and pesticides used in the development process were harmful to the fauna of the rivers.

New era kids will not experience the joys of shrimp catching and swimming in the rivers. They won't know the delight of running into sugarcane fields and eating sweet sugarcane.

What Comes Next?

The time came when I grew up and needed to attend secondary school, which meant more studies. I was quite frustrated, but I managed to complete my secondary studies and was given the opportunity to pursue further education at a full-time university. I did not accept. The reason was simple for me.

Had I enrolled in a university, my mother would have had to bear all the costs involved for my course. She would have been compelled to keep the cow for some three or four years to help pay my university expenses. So, instead I decided to be independent. I wanted to help my parents financially and show them my gratitude. This decision was an important turning point in my life.

With the help of some relatives, I got a job as timekeeper in a construction company. I started to earn my living and worked in the company for some months. I remember that upon receiving my first salary, I went to my mother and handed the complete sum over to her. She shed tears of joy.

I could see how proud my mother was. She turned the money away and told me, "Son, I love you. Keep striving and keep going on. We as parents always want what is best for you." This statement clearly demonstrates my parents' love for their children.

Becoming an Employee

After some years, I got a job at an insurance company. I found the work interesting because it involved dealing with members of the public. Working in this company reminded me of the days when I sold milk for my family. I learnt how to relate to customers through that early experience. Joining the insurance company made me who I am today. I created my own destiny and my own luck and became the Chief Technical Officer.

While working, I also continued studying. I enrolled in open and distance learning programs. Along with a lot of work responsibilities and pressure carrying out several simultaneous projects, studying and concentrating became difficult. But I did not let go and did not allow discouragement to get at me. I kept my motivation high. I remembered the sacrifices my parents made, which inspired me to keep going.

Years passed by and my investments began to pay off. I worked hard, enduring sleepless nights for my studies and my work. I kept on striving and the outcome was fruitful.

Meanwhile, I met my soulmate. She boosted my motivation level to work harder. My house was completed with the help of my in-laws after my wedding. Shandya, my loving wife, supported me and backed me up all the time, and always helped me pursue my dreams. She never let go of me. She stood by me through thick and thin.

Lessons Learned

I believe that you build your own empire with your efforts, confidence, enthusiasm, and willingness to struggle. Success is not attained easily in life. You work for it from the very beginning without even knowing that your prior actions will materialize into your current status.

A flashback takes me to the little kid who was adventurous and full of life. At a tender age, that little guy endured a lot of pain. But he never stopped believing. He dreamt big and desired to achieve.

I kept learning throughout my journey. It all began at a young age when I realized that nothing comes easy in life. Core ingredients such as hard work mixed with tolerance and patience are vital to pursuing success.

Perfection is not guaranteed. Early on, I grasped the essence and importance of perseverance, sacrifices, and patience. I suffered through bullying from families and friends, which toughened my personality.

The experience of being on the outside also helped me not to be judgmental of others or hesitant to help people in any possible way I can. I worked hard and sacrificed further studies to financially help my loving parents. I also fought to protect my sisters.

My relationship and desire to help my sisters, my education, and my first work experiences taught me that nothing is obtained easily in life. You must work your soul and body to the maximum. You must endure pain. You will get knocked down but at the end of the day, victory will triumph.

One core lesson I learned is to never let go. Face your fears and all the odds. Your life choices define you, so make good ones. Figure out what you really want to achieve in life, dream it, and do it.

CHAPTER 3

Understand Yourself

"Success follows doing what you want to do. There is
no other way to be successful." - Malcolm S. Forbes

How will you decide what you want to do? Some people already know the answer while others are still grappling with the question. Knowing what you are created to be is one of the most important things you will ever discover about yourself. It is the first step to achieving success in life.

Let me make something clear at this juncture. For many people, success means having a high-paying job or thriving business, lots of money in a bank account, a marriage to the man or woman of their dreams, beautiful children, and vacations to exotic locations all over the world.

These are good signs of success, but studies have also shown people having all the aforementioned to still feeling a void and lack of fulfillment within them.

I discovered my own path. I will outline the practical steps I took in subsequent chapters for you, in case you are still grappling with your success-step questions. I have experienced firsthand the feelings of total failure. Afterwards, I developed into a successful professional, blazing trails and achieving all that I set out to accomplish.

There are around 7.5 billion people (as of July 2019) in the world. I would say that since we each have our own story, states of mind and approaches, we could easily reach approximately 7.5 billion different profiles. No person is born as a copy of another. We are all unique and we hold different points of view.

My vision of success may be different from your opinion about achieving success. The great Arnold Schwarzenegger stated:

> "Have a vision. Yes. Your own vision. Think big. Think outside the box and get out of your comfortable zone. Don't be afraid to walk the extra mile. Work hard and ignore naysayers, who are none other than energy vampires rather than uplifting people. Choose wisely the type of people you want to have in your friends' circle. Finally, always help people because remember, the blessings of people are more powerful than you may ever think is possible."

Based on the former California governor's statements, it is crystal clear that success is not an easy achievement. As a matter of fact, achieving success demands not only putting Arnold's advice into practice, but starting all over again when life knocks you down.

You must maintain the courage to stand up with even more determination than before.

Reading your own profile

Have you ever stared at yourself in a mirror and wondered, "Why was I born? Why am I even here on this planet?" Have you ever thought about the resolution of your life? Have you achieved something? Have you created positive impact in this world? Do people really like you? So many questions and yet so few answers.

These questions have crossed the minds of so many people. The answers can't be found in any old textbook. Instead, the answers are grasped from life experiences, your parents' guidance, moral values, and the work you put in to conquering your dreams. The effort gives meaning to your life, which could be as simple as finding peace of mind or reaching self-actualization.

Creating Your Roadmap

Our life does not come with a green card or a well-defined roadmap that enables us to freely move everywhere, any place at any time, without bothering about unhappiness. The choices we make, the harshness we endure, and the sacrifices we overcome tend to give our lives true significance. Draw from your experiences—what did you learn from them about the world? More importantly, what did you learn about yourself? This self-reflection helps draw pictures of our lives, guiding us on a path to ascertain what we want to attain, and what our priorities are.

Speaking about priority, I shall bounce back to the time I was eight. At this very young age, I was able to identify my priorities. I made sure my father got home safe, that my sisters were protected, and that my mom had enough grass cuttings. I aided my family by selling milk. These were among my priorities. Now if you can imagine, I did not have anyone at that time to encourage me to follow the path I decided to choose. I wanted to help my family any way that I could, and in doing various things in service to them, I found my path to success.

You are the reason for your success. Unknowingly, you have been nurturing that special seed of your own success that will bloom into your amazing achievement and making you a happy and complete person. Life can be difficult, it can put obstacles in your way, but no matter what you endure, try to find the strength within to grab hold of the situation and work constructively and expectantly.

Find ways to turn any situation in your favor. Embrace your destiny with open arms, and destiny will hug you back with an abundance of joy. As Doug Firebaugh[2] said, "Every day, do something that will inch you closer to a better tomorrow." The decision to work towards happiness or remain idle is ours.

---

[2] Author, Radio Talk Show Host, Success Leadership, and Home Business Trainer.

I strongly believe that everyone in every nook and corner of the world has a specific role and purpose to serve on this planet. Whatever we do will undoubtedly have an impact on someone's life.

For example, imagine a cleaner working hard to earn his living by cleaning the public toilet daily. The public toilet is spotlessly clean when he's finished. He does a tremendous job, which brings satisfaction to the people for having been able to use a clean public toilet.

Now, let us analyze the same scenario from a different angle. The members of the public, after answering the calls of nature, do not bother to keep the toilet clean. Extreme, suffocating smells and urine stains litter the toilet. There is paper and trash scattered everywhere.

We can clearly witness that these acts of the public will have a negative impact on the cleaner's daily routine. Our actions—even ones that seem so small—impact society. It is our role to choose wisely and think well prior to any action we do.

Unlimited Capacity

Let us analyze some of the questions that may emanate from our minds. Are we in control of our destiny? Do we do things that really make us happy or are we currently where we really want to be?

These questions will undoubtedly give rise to many debates. The answers are found in different schools of thought. From falling to getting back on my feet, I draw lessons from the different challenges that I have encountered in my life.

Our life outcomes are tied to the choices we make and the experiences we have. From the very beginning, I wanted to know what the purpose of life was. What I am supposed to do with my life? Numerous questions cropped up in my young mind.

Arnold Schwarzenegger was one of my role models. At a young age, he too struggled to find a purpose. Little did he know that his future included winning the Mr. Olympia contest seven times in a row. He could not predict a future of playing major roles in Hollywood movies on his way to becoming one of the highest paid movie stars.

Though he didn't imagine life as a celebrity, he never thought small, even as a small kid. He had a big vision that goes back to when he was only seven years old. His path was not clear or easy, but with tolerance, patience, confidence, and perseverance, slowly but surely, he was able to materialize his dreams.

Lessons Learned

Life is as complex as a puzzle game of one million pieces that needs to be sorted, assembled, and pieced together to reveal a beautiful and stunning result. This is no easy task. Our lives have a user manual. We just need learn how to read it.

I've learned that we should refuse selfishness in life. We must always think about others. It can be easy to be preoccupied with ourselves, but we should always strive to remember what Confucius stated: "What you do not want done to yourself, do not do to other." We may not be able to predict our future, but we can be certain that big dreams, perseverance, and kindness to others will yield results.

CHAPTER 4

See Possibility in Everything

"It's never crowded along the extra mile." – Dr Wayne Dyer

Anything is possible the day you decide to make it happen, no matter what it is. I strongly believe that everybody can be a doer. God is a creator and since we are made in His image and likeness, we are co-creators with Him. It is embedded in us to create, to build, and to bring things to life from nothingness. But sadly, many people do not realize this and are not living up to their full potential.

Many others erroneously first think, "What's in it for me?" They should be thinking, "What value can I bring to the table? How can I ensure that people part from me feeling more blessed and empowered than they were before they met me?"

Risk is Involved

Life is unpredictable. You must always expect the unexpected because everything is possible. You must create your own plan for the future. Life does not come prepackaged for your convenience.

For one second, imagine you love someone. If you really appreciate that person, you will accept and cherish every facet of them to the utmost, right? But you will agree with me that you cannot fully experience that emotion until that person is willing to share every feeling with you, too.

If you really want to get close to that potential soulmate, you must take risks. You must put yourself out there. You'll likely ask yourself, "is the risk too big to take?"

Foregoing the risk could cause you to miss out on amazing experiences and fulfilling emotions. Love and relationships come directly from the heart.

Now, imagine you are planning to have a baby. Certainly, you do have a lot of books and specialized doctors to guide you on the measures and precautions to take from conception to pregnancy until the delivery and even after your child is born. Our parents may share their experience, but no mother has ever given birth to a baby who comes with a list of his/her functions, scheduled times for feeding, or translated baby language. Having a baby is another high-risk, high-reward proposition we face in life.

With these two examples, I simply mean to say that anything worth having in life comes with inevitable risk. There's no way around; you must choose to be brave and face them head on.

The Human Brain: the 10% myth

Do we really use only 10% of our brain? Many reports have been disputed and reframed by others, but they offer a point of departure for our discussion.

With only 10% utilization, we human beings create wonders. Imagine what we could achieve if we utilized 100% brain capacity.

Is this even possible? How do we know the capacity of our brain or its utilization? The 2014 movie *Lucy*, starring Scarlett Johansson, gave an answer through fiction. Mastering 100% of the character's brain capacity enabled her to perform miracles like time travel and advanced foresight among various other phenomena. Personally, I am comfortable with my current brain capacity. It has enabled me to be where I currently am. But the prospect does say something about human capabilities for greatness.

I have read dozens of books on success and motivation. Most have a common denominator: our mental attitude. Our mind, our motivation, and mental approach can result in miracles. If we can control our mind to keep our motivation level high, we can be capable of achieving many things.

For example, the lifestyle of monks reveals the power of mental acuity. Their discipline and dedication are astonishing. With a deep breath and unflinching concentration, a monk can easily endure a brutal blow of a sledgehammer on their stomach without betraying a single flinch of pain.

The monks did not develop this capacity overnight. It takes many years of practice. The ability to master the power of the mind as taught to the monks is critical to their enhanced ability.

One of the most important things that you should train your mind to do is to let go of anything that was not meant to be and move to the next level. Wesley Snipes stated: "Ninety-percent of what you are stressing over today won't even be relevant in some time; so, breathe easy."

Your Plan, People and Possibilities

Larry Winget said: "Nobody ever wrote down a plan to be broke, fat, lazy, or stupid. Those things are what happen when you don't have a plan." This valuable assertion should be a caution against flying blind. Create your plan based upon who you are at your core. Complete your tasks on your terms and pursue a plan based on your dreams. Let your dreams speak a thousand words to you but grab one of those words. Go for it. Work your soul for it. Remember, the winners and achievers are those who never gave up despite having tasted many failures.

Some people embrace changes and demonstrate flexibility. They accept challenges and will fight against all wrongs. They never let go. They keep on striving and refuse to let the fear of failing prevent them from being happy. Those people allow themselves to fall, hurt, but always garner enough courage and determination to rise stronger.

These people learn lessons from their mistakes and failures. They work hard to remedy mistakes. They exercise adaptability in the face of changes. They know that everything happens for a reason, and they are always ready to welcome challenges.

Many people view life as being tough or difficult. Unfortunately, these people never see positives. They hold sadness and disappointment like trophies. Their stress level is at a constant mercurial rise. They tend to develop an aptitude for luring people into their negativity and nurture a knack for absorbing positive energy from other people. Being unhappy with their lives, they are usually frustrated and never find any good in anything. They interact only through complaint and have no peace of mind.

What is more unfortunate is that these people are not happy to see you happy. They will envy you and will be vested with jealousy. These people stoop low to hurt your feelings. One saying reported by Sacagawea reads: "People who are intimidated by you, talk bad about you with hopes that others won't find you so appealing". This perfectly applies to the individuals we just described. Throughout my career, I have come across many such people.

On the other hand are people who see life as a big adventure. They are daredevils and look insatiably for the next adrenaline rush. They never encounter "life in recession" or depression. They have everything that they could ever imagine. Those materialistic things, in their minds, ensure their happiness. They live a utopian lifestyle whereby superficial comparison determines value.

One great example of this type of person in popular culture is the one and only Lex Luthor (Michael Rosenbaum) from the television series *Smallville.* He is addicted to ruling the world. He is a billionaire, owns many prestigious sports cars, lives in a splendid mansion, has millions of dollars invested in real estate, and lives a lavish lifestyle. He has the capacity to afford what he owns. There is nothing wrong in that.

His best friend is Clark Kent (Tom Welling), a humble farm boy who leads his life in a simple manner alongside his parents and friends. Lex Luthor misses these relationships the most in his life. His father's drive for money led to a poor father-son relationship. He lost his mother at a young age, and he is always engulfed in his next move to conquer the business world. In the end, Lex Luthor admits that what he misses the most is a humble and life with loving parents and friends.

This scenario prompts a couple questions. Will these people be able to bear a disruption in their life? Will they have what it takes to bear sadness or depression? Probably not, as they've never experienced it in a real way. The answer will be a big no.

Lessons Learned

Success and happiness in your life begin with seeing possibilities. You must determine the risks you are willing to take, build your mental preparation, and plan your life decisions in the most authentic and efficient manner.

I therefore recommend what has worked well for me. Do your best and the rewards will follow. Sit and decide within yourself, what you desire to bless humanity with and get going. The complete process of how to proceed from there will unfold gradually before you as you take the first step.

Clarity occurs on the journey and remember—destiny is not a destination—it is a journey. When you have decided to start on your journey, give 100% and expect 0%. The greater rewards will come soon.

I am very satisfied about where I have reached now. I am pleased to have gone through a lot of ups and downs, to finally gain the ability to grasp success. Life is a never-ending quest of happiness and success. All you must do is keep on believing and never ever underestimate the power of your mind and willingness.

You are very special in your own ways. You have gifted talents and your limit is absolutely boundless. You must believe in yourself, set free of all the worries and negativity, get hold of challenges, and strive to the utmost.

Resist any limits in pursuing your dreams. You can do stunningly beautiful things in your life. Just think where you currently are now. You surely have come one step forward from where you were yesterday.

All it took was a little courage, a helping of determination, and a dose of willpower. Do not ever let anyone keep your key to happiness in their possession. Write you own destiny with your own ink and be proud of your failures and successes. After all, it is your life, your story, and your success.

Walking Through
the Adult Lessons

I further thought, if now I deny
Those that would have it, thus to gratify,
I did not know but hinder them I might
Of that which would to them be great delight."
-*The Pilgrim's Progress*

CHAPTER 5

Pay the Price

"If you want to achieve a high goal, you're going to
have to take some chances." – Alberto Salazar

I am sure you have noticed people with designer suits, expensive cars, plush offices, large houses, and above-standard lifestyles while walking around or travelling. We sometimes think, "How lucky they are! God is favoring them!"

We fail to realise the trail that they travelled to arrive at that position. I am not talking about people who use shortcuts to get to where they are today. I am referring to all those who genuinely, through toil and sacrifice, work for their success.

We always want to achieve more, but we don't always realise that we need to leave our comfort zones and apply extra effort to do so. Extra effort also means focus. Focusing means putting aside other tasks in favor of the current priority.

What I am trying to demonstrate is that there will always be a compromise. Jack Canfield mentioned this reality in his book, *The Success*

Principles. Canfield says, "Be willing to pay the price." Sometimes, you know in advance the price you will have to pay. Other times, it comes as a surprise.

Sometimes, you are prepared to pay. Other times, you are at a loss for how you will cover the expense. My price to pay came as a surprise. I learned some important lessons to help you ensure that you see the costs coming.

My mission is to make you aware that there is a price to pay to get where you want to be. You need to get ready for it. When you are ready, it is easier because you are mentally comfortable with the change.

Joining the Group

After working for two previous companies, I received an offer to work for another company. I was young and desired to grow in my career. My networking was critical.

At the time I received the offer, I was an active member of the Insurance Institute. I was among those always ready to help and this is where I met some influential people in the insurance industry. I was very timid with an inferiority complex towards others. Maybe it was due to my upbringing and childhood environment.

After completing three interviews, I was retained. This was the best company to work for. I knew that joining this company would put me on a great path. I informed a colleague about the option and he told me, "You will make money there, but you will also sacrifice your family time. You know what time you start each workday, but you never know when the workday will end."

Money was important to me at that time. I came from a poor family, I was newly married and needed to leave my family's dependence and construct my house. I was willing to pay the price of family time at that age to devote more of my time to the company.

The next change came in 2000, when I received a call from the conglomerate's Operations Manager. He said that I had been referred by a common friend, Mr. Clarel Marie and continued saying that he was looking for someone to assist me on a project. I attended the first interview and was called for a second one. After one additional interview, I was finally selected.

Some years back, I had applied to the same company but was not selected for the job. I seized the opportunity to ask the Managing Director the reason for not being hired at that time. He told me that the company does not recruit people who want to leave their current position. He explained that the company recruits people who are satisfied with their job. In this way, they are confident that they'll get the right person who is mentally and professionally stable. He added that they create a supportive environment for the person and a pathway to enhanced success. I was amazed by this way of recruitment. In fact, the position I occupied was higher than the one I applied for some years back. Luckily, I was not selected at that time as I don't believe I would have reached the position where I am today.

My Progress

I started as a Unit Leader and gradually moved on to Project Manager, Operations Manager, Vice President, Senior Vice President, Deputy CEO in Botswana, and now Chief Technical Officer. Rather than listing all these titles to impress you, I list them, as my mentor Jack Canfield said, to impress *upon* you that if you decide definitively and give your best, anything is possible. My growth was mainly due to building up my self-confidence by increasing my self-esteem.

This same self-confidence has given me opportunities to speak in Ghana and has allowed me to travel to Nigeria as a consultant and organize the Success Principles in Botswana and Mauritius. Once you start to shine, you are visible from far away, and you attract success.

Another thing that has worked for me in this regard is the ability to boldly showcase myself. Prior to the time I went through experiences that helped me to truly discover myself, I was a very timid person. I wasn't self-aware, and had a hard time relating to people. I didn't know how to express myself well and faced difficulty channeling my energies.

As a package of constraints, I knew that these would prevent me from reaching the height I wanted no matter how hard I tried. I knew that I had to change these traits. Indeed, when things changed my life changed.

People's perception of me changed. I began to reap the success that I envisioned for myself.

After joining the group, I was assigned various projects to carry out. I was used to working on one task at a time but with the new company, I was often asked to multitask. I observed people coming in early and staying late to prove themselves. I was not used to this and found out that performance was tied to bonuses. I needed money and was motivated to progress.

I once asked my supervisor, "Which project is the priority?" And he answered, "Each one is the priority. None is less than the others."

Previously, I was able to go home and relax after work. For six months in the company, I experienced no rest, even after work. *Welcome to the real corporate world!* I could not relax as my mind was struggling through problems, tasks, and multiple projects focused on progressing. I had to come home and continue working.

One major project was reviewing the filling in of documents and the Insurance Software. Luckily, I had some experience in project management. With the help of a few colleagues, I managed to bring forth something which we could all be proud of. This was also the beginning of my life as a travelling professional. I spent a few weeks in London with the developers. Slowly, I was experiencing the corporate environment. I became more confident with time.

Once the project completed, I was appointed Operations Manager. I was offered my first company car. This was really a turning point, a sense of pride, and what I considered success.

Success is not a permanent destination. After achieving one success, you instinctively crave another. Slowly, I set a few other goals such as completing my diploma in Insurance, securing my MBA, and progressing further in the company. The group was always re-engineering and new blood joined the company. I was asked to take up a new position and left Life Operations, a department in which I was more comfortable.

Picasso and Me

My son Jihan was born the same year I joined the new company. To prove myself, I assumed a tremendous amount of responsibility. I was working very hard and barely spent time with my little boy. My colleague's warning echoed loudly. I still remember the night when Jihan was playing, and he wanted something. Looking at me, he called me "mum". This is when I realized the first price I paid on my journey to success. I quickly climbed the ladder in the company due to my work ethic, but it came at a price.

I remember Picasso's famous story used in many motivational workshops by famous speakers. He was walking down the street and was stopped by a lady who requested that he make a painting for her. Picasso took barely 30 seconds to make a painting and handed it over to the lady. She thanked him, but Picasso told her, "It will cost you $1,000,000."

Surprised, the lady replied, "Mr. Picasso, this is not fair. It took you only 30 seconds, and you are asking for $1,000,000. How?"

Picasso smiled and stated, "My dear lady, it took me 30 years to be where I am today." [3]

Picasso also paid a price to be where he was at the time of the lady's request. Sometimes, paying the price may be to the detriment of your family and other things. But you will have to pay the price to be a success. To be successful, you need to be well-trained, disciplined, and prepared to sacrifice in the short-term to achieve your long-term desire.

Health and Body

Paying the price may also result in not taking care of your body and health. When you are working on a project, you tend to unconsciously focus on it to the exclusion of other tasks. You work long hours and may forget about taking care of your health.

These habits affect your outcomes. These are not costs that you want to pay for extended periods. You should strive to adopt healthy habits. You should shore up the discipline required to maintain a long-term flexibility even during the short-term intensity.

When you are not in the office, you should set an out-of-office message. It makes sense to balance the sacrifice across multiple areas like you do with the out-of-office message. One technique is scheduling time for each of your priorities. Explain to your family that your period of engagement is limited.

---

[3] The anecdote about Picasso

When you are engaged, be present in what you are doing. You can't go to the gym and spend the whole time on your phone. You have many people sitting on the machines looking, chatting, and engrossed with their phones. Some of them are just listening to music, but others are spending half of the time on their phones. They were supposed to be working out their muscles, but they are exercising their thumbs!

This brings up another concern. It is not just to show off or to post a selfie that you were in the gym. You must pay the price of growth and development for the task at hand. If you exercise in the gym, you will feel the pain of that workout. Eventually, the result is physical health. You must be willing to pay that price of pain to realize the gains.

Lessons Learned

The lesson I learned was to always have faith in God and be patient. I also learned that I need to be conscious of the kind of vibes I send out in my work. I have witnessed people who complain daily, inconsolably about their work. I have noticed that such people do not excel at their jobs. Their performance and competence suffer. The dividends of the job never accrue to them.

Jack Canfield always says, "Pain is only temporary. The benefits last forever." Students sacrifice sleep and leisure time to obtain good grades. Sales personnel sacrifice family time to meet new prospects. Businesspeople sacrifice savings to invest in their businesses.

They each do this for one reason, to be successful and achieve their dreams. I sacrificed almost three years not spending time with my son for professional reasons. I am not asking you to do the same, but only making you aware that you will have to pay a price to be successful. During those days, my wife was the only one to look after Jihan. I was also sacrificing time spent with her.

To be honest, I was not prepared for that. After reading *The Success Principles* for the first time, I realised that I paid a tangible price to be where I am today. You will improve upon my experience if you acknowledge well ahead the price you will pay to reach your goal. I would rather that you take note of the costs and prepare your success plan, therefore limiting your potential dissatisfaction.

Some have had trouble completing a project because they changed their routine too much. They did not consider their health, family, and routine in the formula. Some may describe this as a balanced life. I see it as difficult to consider it as a "balance." You pay the price of not sleeping, spending time with the family, or the quality of work you complete.

In the 24 hours you have, you must be organized. There will be sacrifices but you can make these more manageable. You may end up sacrificing sleep, quality time, or exercise to work on the project. No matter what it is, you will definitely be sacrificing something. Many limit themselves because they are not willing to do this.

College students seem to have an easier time with this. They need to pass the exam, so they sacrifice sleep time to study. Perhaps the context and environment suggest that this is the appropriate behavior for them. Other environments may not offer the same guidance. You must set the priorities and make the choices for yourself.

CHAPTER 6

Find Purpose in Setbacks

"If you want to be happy, set a goal that commands your thoughts, liberates your energy, and inspires your hopes." – Andrew Carnegie

In Mauritius, it is often and fallaciously assumed that foreigners can do better than the locals, but it is not always meant with sinister intent. International exposure can also be good for corporate images, but it can also get in the way of local people's success. For example, a new COO was recruited from abroad to take up the position I held. I was asked to take a different position which was newly created. I had to take the job against my will. I oversaw Operations and maybe the company was not seeing my worth.

I occupied a position as Business & Channel Development and was entrusted responsibility to develop new channels for sales. Being an operations person, business development was not my cup of tea. I asked myself whether this was a strategy to get rid of me. I was in the back office previously, and now, I found myself in a sales position on the front line.

I started by reading up on sales and business development. My first assignment was visiting all the health centres with a colleague to communicate the value-add of our business through product posters and engagement. I was driving many kilometres to multiple centres around the island. I benefitted from the time exploring the country, but I was not enjoying the job. I also had a hard time communicating about what I was doing. I felt that people in the company would soon question the value of my position.

On the Edge of Suicide

I was completely disoriented and not feeling valuable or productive. My subconscious mind was on the brink of a breakdown. I recall one day, I hit the brakes in the middle of the road. I started screaming to let go of my stress. The primal release seemed to work for a moment, but then I felt overwhelmed again.

The same week, I returned home after a day's work. Sitting in front of the television, my attention was elsewhere. I was contemplating suicide as the pain, pressure, and stress were unbearable. I am not sure where the dark thoughts came from. I imagined myself dropping from my seat. The demon on my left shoulder was saying, "Just die by committing suicide. You are not moving forward."

I think the angel on my right shoulder was more powerful. He simply showed me the picture of my wife and son. I reasoned myself that I could not just escape from the problems. *What about my son? Who is going to provide for his education? What about my wife?*

My Wife as Savior

Thoughts of my wife and son called me back to the responsibilities that I am happy to shoulder. I decided to accept my new position at work and commit to the daily tasks. I shared my challenges with my wife. She was characteristically supportive and positive and advised me to be patient. "Your time will come one day," she said.

Without her guidance and support, I believe I would have died by suicide. My wife is strong and can manage multiple problems. She always has a balanced mindset. She said, "This is part of life. Be patient. Maybe you are being tested by God. This will forge your character and make you stronger."

"Do whatever you are told to do and do the right thing," I told myself. "If you are honest and hardworking, you will reclaim what you enjoy doing. Use this circumstance to explore what it means to be an extrovert. Maybe this will take you out of your introverted comfort zone."

On the Road

I had a few questions: *What is my challenge? What is depressing me?* The answers were connected to my work. Maybe I was upset because I did not know how to do it. How do you learn how? Read, watch videos, and attend trainings. My road to acceptance was a series of questions on one side and a wide range of answers on the other. I chose to focus on connecting questions to answers.

If you want to be an expert, read on the subject you want to master every week. In five years, you will be an expert. This is what I began to do. I watched many videos related to sports—people surpassing themselves. Everything that holds you back or propels you forward resides in your mind. You have both a conscious mind and a subconscious mind.

You control how the connections are established in your mind. If you connect your situation to despair and unhappiness through complaining, this pattern will be anchored within your brain. That will be what you think of and how you perceive the situation. On the other hand, if you practice gratitude and identify silver linings through thank yous and bright sides, your brain will default to these settings. What is amazing is this change in your perspective changes your behaviour. Together, they change your experience of life.

I started working on myself. I refused to complain and I began to work this situation to my benefit. I read books on sales and started to gain expertise in my area. Not only books about sales and communication, but also human behaviour, mindfulness, becoming, and self-development.

I established a new norm for myself. I believe this is what led me to the Success Principles.

I knew my skills and competencies. I was developing them rather than lamenting any deficit. A lot of mess existed in the company policies and procedures that required attention. I had to get those on track to support what I now knew was best practice in the field. I reached agreements on process and a level of balance with the help of the team. I engaged and reclaimed my value as someone the company could count on.

Rediscovering My Why: My Family

Somewhere down memory lane is a child always being teased, tagged as uneducated, and introverted. This haunted me when I focused on the negatives of my life. I did not realize that the experience was like medication, which is often bitter and not sweet. It is important because it makes you better. Maybe this was an opportunity to learn from something bitter, taking it and allowing it to develop my character.

I was determined to work out my life's purpose and get myself on track to be who I was created to be. The past was still relevant but used in a positive sense rather than a negative sense. I was dedicated and had a goal which is to take care of my family.

Each step you take is moving you toward your goal or away from your goal. My previous choice was to take the pressure and weight on my shoulders weighed down by my past. For me, it was like a car that is out of alignment. I had to realign myself to focus on happiness and the "why" of my life. This put me on the right track. I was able to progress straight toward my success.

I heard myself telling my son, "All the people who are alone die early." For me, family is part of your reason to be alive. I made a decision to get married and then to have children.

You have choices as well. Once you choose to do something, purpose develops. At the time of my suicidal thoughts, the "why" of my family led to the rediscovery of my reason for being. That kept me alive. From there, I began to look at what I needed to do to develop into my best self, regardless of the situation.

Your own obituary. What will people say when you are gone? Will they just note that you are gone? Or, will they discuss how deeply you are missed because of the things you achieved, the way you marked their lives, the encouragement you gave them, the risk you took, and the heights you strived toward? I did this, and saw for myself all of my accomplishments. This has helped me to encourage myself and move toward my life's purpose.

Lessons Learned

It was a few years before I was called back into operations. My wife continued to motivate me throughout the process, always believing that I would be restored to my old job. As if my wife had a crystal ball, the company did call me back to operations. From that moment, I began to tell people that everything happens for a reason. You have no red carpet. You must make your way. You create the trail. You blaze a trail for others.

Now, I thank God that I had this experience. Owing to this, I obtained expertise in sales *and* operations. I experienced a good mix of leadership and back office as well as client engagement.

The experiences that you sometimes dread and lament are tests to deepen your interest and passion for your life's purpose. With this, you will move forward and create your trail no matter what happens. See them as part of the process. Not up or down, but ever forward.

Life will present challenges that are not meant to hurt but in fact are being deliberately set to make you grow and become strong. Always have a purpose in your life and make the purpose the reason for you to stay alive. Had I not thought of my family, I would have been no more by now. Stay put with your objectives no matter what.

Write your story holding your own pen. Do not allow others to hold the pen. If you want to be successful, be aware of these challenges you'll have to face.

Commit to growth. This life is the only one you have. Own it. *Grow through* all the circumstances instead of *going through* them. What you become in the process is what matters. I became more mature and learned how to handle difficult situations. I understood the importance of surrounding myself with family. This experience prepared me to succeed in my next challenge.

Remain happy no matter what. Being happy does not just mean that you smile and laugh more or that you find everything that you do pleasurable. Happiness entails more than that. Positive emotions are only one aspect of happiness. Your life's circumstances do not need to determine whether you are happy. That is not all that matters. What matters is how you react to your circumstances. When you are intentionally happy, it reflects in your outlook on life and in the work that you do. Positive engagement, purpose and meaning, and positive relationships; these are the reflections of happiness.

Positive engagement occurs when an individual is so fully engrossed in what he or she is doing that they lose track of time. They are in the "flow." This ultimately means that if you are in the flow with any activity that you are engaged in, you will be more productive and feel the rewards of engagement.

Develop purpose and meaning. When people believe in what they are doing, they feel a greater sense of fulfillment and life satisfaction. Accomplishment is very important in experiencing satisfaction in life. When you strive to achieve your goals and show determination when enduring tough times, you will feel more fulfilled.

Experiencing positive relationships is another important factor promoting excellence. Having a friend at school or on your team at work will surely account for a stronger sense of belonging. You will feel more relevant. You will likely commit further in such an environment.

CHAPTER 7

Grow with Opportunities

"You've got to ask! Asking is, in my opinion, the world's most powerful—and neglected—secret to success and happiness." — Percy Ross

After several years, a new employee joined the company and I was requested to share my duties. I took over the technical aspect of the operations and was appointed Vice President of Technical Services.

A few months later, I encountered some conflicts with one of my colleagues and decided to hand over everything to her. I moved to Business and Channel Development full time. This began my first exposure to sales.

I made this decision with positive expectations as I was already prepared for change—after all, I'd already experienced it. This time I chose the job. With the support of my reporting line, I knew I would be able to deliver. Well, I believed I was ready. However, in practice I had a few challenges. Part of my role was holding weekly motivational sales meetings with 750+ salespersons. Initially, I was mentored alongside my reporting line. But after two months, I was on my own.

Finding My Voice

I recall one of the first meetings. Afterwards, one of my colleagues commented that I should speak as if I was on one side of a football stadium, trying to speak to someone on the other side. In other words, my voice was too low and people at the back of the room could not hear me. Initially, I didn't appreciate the remark, because he made it in front of my other colleagues.

However, I took it seriously and started to search for courses on public speaking. I came across a company in Johannesburg that offered some options. I contacted The Voice Clinic to explore the courses available. Unfortunately, I was told that I needed to travel for a one-day course. After working out the figures, it turned out to be expensive as I needed to arrange for travel and hotel accommodations.

I desperately wanted to attend this training. I made a request that they conduct the training via Skype. They agreed for 8 one-hour sessions. I believe I was the first one who followed the course via Skype. They soon included this option in their catalog.

When I was holding sales meetings, I was monotonous and this was difficult for people listening. At the same time, shouting while delivering a speech or motivational talk can be offensive. I learned instead that there are different tones and pitches to use when giving a speech.

I learned to utilize the nose, throat, and diaphragm. Your eyes gaze toward four points of vision routinely when talking. You look right, left, middle, and back. Rather than looking only at the person who is comfortable and responsive, cast your gaze to pre-identified anchor points. I learned to worry less about the audience and more about my own preparation. Keywords, quotes, and illustrations became comfortable for me to include in my presentation.

I began to apply the lessons in three general sales meetings each week. I learned to present 80% of the information on slides and 20% by improvising based on interactions with my audiences. Repeating a presentation can be challenging. People can make out whether you have talked about the same content over and over. I began to derive pleasure from connecting specifically to the audience. This led me on the path to desiring certification as a motivational speaker.

I rehearsed the speaking techniques I learned and slowly managed to speak loud enough so that people at the back of the hall could hear me. From there, I continued my journey in Business & Channel Development for four years. Thanks to this experience, I was selected finalist for the British Excellence Sales Management Awards 2011 as Sales Director of the Year. I travelled to few countries with the winners of our Sales Convention. I visited India, Brazil, USA, and also had the opportunity to experience a European Cruise.

Sales Overseas

My exposure to sales opened up more opportunities. After spending some years in Sales, I was entrusted responsibility to work on an overseas project. My task was to open a branch in Botswana. I was appointed project manager and presented with an option to move to Botswana to start operations. I was selected based on my exposure to both operations and sales.

The set up was off to a solid start with the help of the project team. Following the initial success, the day arrived that I had to move. Though it was a smooth transition, there was no red-carpet reception.

I finally settled in Gaborone after finding a house, buying a car, and more. I was seconded as the Deputy CEO/Principal Officer. I had to quickly acclimate and understand a new culture to make things work.

My situation in Mauritius was not the same as in Gaborone. I had to be very patient, but I was blessed to have had good colleagues with good attitudes who only needed guidance. Despite my title, I found myself having to vacuum the office on the eve of the launch as the team was confused as to why this had to be done. For them, the state of the office was okay, but not for me. As the Chairman and guests of honor would attend the launch, the office needed to be immaculate.

In the initial month, it was challenging working with the CEO, who was a local lady. I felt I was not receiving proper respect. In one instance, she openly mentioned that I was not the right person for the job and that the locals did not trust me. This was said in a board meeting, and I was surprised at such remarks.

My friend, Ntshiwa, another local, was helping me a lot to settle in and always encouraging me to be patient. This new adventure was a turning point in my career. I learned to be independent for some time without my extended family.

Turning Point Explained

Everything happens for a reason. I was selected to work in Botswana because of the exposure I had within the company. This was a turning point in my life and career. This international exposure changed my personality. *"What does not kill you, makes you stronger…"* The lyrics of Pink's song, "Try," were my motivation. The song boosted me up.

> "Where there is a desire, there's gonna be a flame.
> Where there is a flame, someone's bound to get burned.
> But, because it burns, doesn't mean you're gonna die. You
> gotta get up and try, and try, and try."

I held these lyrics in mind through all the difficulties and kept going. Today, I am burned but alive.

My previous demotion was a learning experience. It is difficult to see the wisdom and opportunity in the moment. I felt at that time like it was unfair and a slap in the face. But the medicine you must take will not always be sweet. This experience made me stronger and ready to tackle the next hurdle in my work life. The challenge for me was that I was forced to take a new position.

I realized, though, that I was lucky. I was able to stay, but I was also able to learn new skills. This made me the right person to be selected for the Botswana project. I learned to talk with people and to negotiate on the fly. I knew the company's culture and DNA. I was tasked with training others on the procedures and our modus operandi. My exposure to different areas of the company, from back office to front office, gave me more perspective on a new job description.

The Almighty knows what He is doing. If I didn't persevere in this area, if I had quit and pursued the idea of staying in my comfort zone, I would have lost the opportunity to travel and grow internationally. My fear of traveling is gone. The experience changed me, but it started with a choice to stick it out.

This is not to say that it wasn't challenging. The experience helped me get ready. When I compare myself to my colleagues, I have a different perspective.

Lessons Learned

Decide what you want and train yourself to raise your level of awareness. To be successful, be ready to leave your comfort zone. As for me, I left my comfortable experience in Life Operations and I took over Sales as a new career opportunity.

I became more confident and less afraid to talk. In fact, I was the emcee for the sales competition launches and the last one was in the presence of the Group Managing Director. Just imagine the stress and the joy after addressing such an accomplished audience. Be prepared if you are not able to take the responsibility. Read up on the subject. Engage a coach or a mentor.

CHAPTER 8

Endure the Crash

"Never give up on your dreams ... Perseverance is all important. If you don't have the desire and the belief in yourself to keep trying after you've been told you should quit, you'll never make it." – Tawni O'Deil

Setup for the Crash

When I started my first job, most parents I knew would suggest that their children join the government sector so that they would have a pension at retirement. Everything would be guaranteed. It was stable employment. This was the goal: to work continuously for a gracious living and a comfortable retirement.

I did not follow that plan. As soon as I finished with my schooling, I was working in the private sector. Instead of staying with the same company consistently until retirement, I changed companies three times. I heard somewhere that you can improve your income and receive promotions more easily if you move every five years. You can also take along your portable pension from one employer to another. I took that advice to heart, wanting to achieve more than what was the norm.

I joined my third company thinking that I would only stay for five years. As you will recall from what I shared in previous sections, my responsibilities increased moving from business to project manager/operations manager. My last position was deputy CEO in Botswana. I was learning a great deal and was exposed to people from multiple cultures and nationalities. I was able to work in and out of Mauritius. I was making progress, growing, and improving professionally. This is how I remained in the company for 15 years.

It was a professional environment that was ripe for growth. Most of the people who worked there planned to continue working until their retirement. I was satisfied with my job. Everything was fine. The pay, travel, latest trends, latest technology were all fantastic. It was a safety and security, but it was also an experience for growth and development. People respected me. What more did I need? For me, the only logical answer was to stay with the company.

When the group crashed, I realized that I needed a plan B. I knew that some employees had side jobs. I was comfortable and did not have a side option. I had put all my eggs into one basket. I should have put my eggs in several baskets. The universe was saying, through the crash, that I needed to work out a plan B. This is what I set about doing.

Arnold Schwarzenegger has been quoted as hating plan Bs. He says that many often forget their plan A when plan B is present. But I don't think his idea applies. Here, I am discussing the scenario of plan A ending with a crash. When plan A is no longer salvageable, you need a plan B to continue forward.

The Company Crash

I started working in the insurance sector 20 years ago. I decided not to enroll at a university. Insurance was not the career I would have chosen, but I needed to obtain a job and get started. This was my first full-time job. I was hired thanks to a relative's help. This was my first encounter with insurance. One of my schoolbooks talked about commerce, stating,

"You cannot conduct any business without insurance." This was my only formal training.

I learned on the job. I understood the difference between types of insurance and discovered I was working in life assurance. I soon passed the exam and obtained a job. I studied with the distance learning school for five years in the first job. I advanced in responsibilities in the second company. I built on insurance expertise and joined the Insurance Institute of Mauritius. I worked on different committees. I met many friends who were pioneers in the industry. I received a reference from a friend to work in the life insurance sector of a new company.

In 2000, I received an offer. This brought a change in my personality and life situation. An ex-employee of the company from which I received an offer told me : "You may have joined the company for money and promotion. You will have to decide how you will pay the price for your family." I trained and traveled with the company. It was a 180 degree turn from my previous experience. I was no longer the timid person who was not comfortable talking in front of a crowd. I was exposed to board meetings. I talked with consultants and other language speakers explaining projects and opportunities. I became a new person.

I got a new car. For the first time, I traveled on annual vacation with my family. My clothing style changed. The company Chairman advised that everything is about your persona and your image. When he would read a book and like it, he would invite the author to speak to the staff. The latter were happy and were well paid. He recognized the value that he could add and that this would keep his staff loyal and provide an anchor to the company. It prevented us from even thinking about moving to another company. We were able to focus on the work toward the vision of the company.

The Chairman convened an annual meeting. Only 50 people from the company were selected to attend. "You need to wake up earlier than your competition. How many of you wake up early?" he asked.

"I wake up early, and I'm in the office by 7:00 am," a guy said, wanting to impress the Chairman. But this wasn't the point that the Chairman was making. He was saying that you need to think and plan. You need to do things that your competitors are not even thinking about.

This was a tasty dish to me. It was an opportunity for change with all the spices of newness. I was selected to work in Botswana as part of our expansion plan. I was able to grow even more and to experience university life without having actually attended a university.

The plan seemed clear to me. After being in Botswana for a while, I was ready to ask for an extension. I saw the vision of the expansion. There was no question that the company would not be around for a long time. I thought about the opportunities while there; about the success and enjoyment I had while motivating and training my sales team.

I read to share during meetings. I considered that I needed some certification to remain credible. I thought about John Maxwell's training. It consisted of 10 sessions that I would have to attend an hour away in Johannesburg. The future, as they say, was bright.

Then, we began to receive "yellow alerts". I started receiving calls from different people warning me to be aware of changes that may result from the outcome of the election. As if they were prophetic, the license of the bank forming part of the group was revoked. This had a major impact on the financials of the insurance company. It was like a bad dream.

Prior to this, everything was fine. I was flying business-class. Suddenly, I was in the middle of a crash. Just as I was about to sign up for the Maxwell certification, the crash of the company occurred. I did not have a clue what was going on. I was telling my son that I would send him to the best universities. "We will be able to afford everything for you," I told him. With the crash of the company came a new environment of uncertainty.

Friday, 3rd April 2015, it was early morning and a public holiday in Botswana. I was in a deep sleep when I heard my phone ringing. My eyes barely open, I held my phone and saw my wife's number. It was still dark outside and in my room. The bright light of the phone was not helping my eyes to adjust. "Have you heard the news? Did someone contact you from Mauritius?"

"No…why?" I replied. "What happened?"

"The bank's license has been revoked by the Central Bank of Mauritius." I jumped out from my bed my eyes wide open.

The bank she was talking about was part of the group for which I worked. Sooner or later, the insurance company would be affected. To add insult to injury, my family held our savings in a fixed deposit with this bank. The savings were for our son's education. It was a shock. I could hear my heart pumping blood faster as stress took over.

It was a long Easter weekend. I had planned for a long drive in the bush with my in-laws and son. I cancelled the trip. The atmosphere around my family suddenly changed from excitement to concern. I informed them about the situation and obviously they got worried too.

I sent a text message to the CEO and few other colleagues in Mauritius. Pin-drop silence best describes the absence of response. I tuned to Mauritius radio channels via the Internet for live news coverage. It was more frustrating as I heard all sorts of news and descriptors of what occurred. "Day light robbery," "Ponzi Scheme," and "Mauritian Madoff" were just a few of the hyperbolic headlines. Police had secured the bank and insurance offices preventing staff from entering the premises.

The government held press conferences to explain the situation. Officials endeavored to reassure bank deposit holders and clients of the insurance company. What I managed to gather from the news was that the revocation resulted from the bank's inability to inject more liquid funds as requested by the Bank of Mauritius. Other private media dissected the reason put forward for this sudden liquidity issue.

According to in-depth reporting, the bank was thrown into the liquidity crisis some time before the start of the month after a few public sector bodies inexplicably withdrew their deposits en masse. Once the bank's license was revoked, this precipitated the downfall of the insurance company.

Finally, the entire group collapsed. The assets of the group were left lying in the hands of two special administrators appointed by the financial regulator, the Financial Services Commission.

Since I had no news from Mauritius, I contacted my current CEO in Botswana to share the news. We met over a cup of coffee and discussed the way forward. We had no other options than to wait and see. Once the local media disseminated the news, things got worse. Clients called incessantly to inquire about their policies. The shares in Botswana were sold off, and I had to return to Mauritius, feeling desperate with a broken dream as I was planning to settle there in the long-term.

The situation had a ripple effect on the institutions of Botswana, on my employer, employed families, my son's education. The financial sector and the country's reputation were damaged. Employees had financial commitments that became precarious. The atmosphere in the country was chaotic. We were not sure whether we would keep our jobs or not.

My son was forced to join another school in Mauritius, starting a new curriculum in the middle of the year. He still had to sit for examinations at the end of the year as if he had been there all along. It was a very challenging time for him and the entire family.

Seeking Solace

A few months later, my company experienced a complete drop in sales. Many clients were surrendering their policies for fear of losing their money. It was also an opportunity for competitors to increase their sales as we were holding more than 50% of the new business shares. All these issues forced the management to make a bold decision. They had to decide whether to reduce staff or reduce our salary. The second option was chosen. In my situation, my total remuneration package was reduced by 55%.

Overnight, I was forced to survive on a reduced salary of only 45% of my usual pay. All other benefits ceased. It was a situation of chaos, also shared by all other staff. What would you do? All the questions rushed through my mind. How would I respect my financial commitments? These questions hung like dark clouds, haunting me daily.

The challenge was that it was the company I had planned on working for and eventually, retiring from. I was not looking for new challenges or experiences. I went up from a junior to a deputy CEO. I was moving forward, consistently seeing myself as the driver of business development in the region. In my mind, the company would excel under my regional development in Africa.

I was focusing on a single lane. There were different challenges in that lane. I was driving on a fast track, straight line. It was like a large lava flow gushing across the road. There was no way to move forward. I had to question what I was going to do. I knew it would take time to fix. It didn't feel like a change or slow down. It felt like the end.

Lessons Learned

I realized that I only had one plan. Reinventing myself began with understanding that I only had a plan A. I did not have a plan B.

I learned to think of new opportunities about moving forward. When I sat down and meditated on my career, I was already on the path toward motivational speaking. I decided to put more energy into that direction. I sought refuge in reading motivational books. Jim Rohn, Tony Robbins, Robin Sharma, Jack Canfield, and others are my sources of wisdom and calm.

My mind went into overdrive, thinking constantly about my next step. First things first, I reviewed all my expenses and reduced them. No more satellite TV or maid service. I cut down on restaurant visits. I thought I would sell my car but could not obtain the right price.

I ended up selling a property to settle the outstanding balance. My wife sold another property to settle a mortgage and reduce our outflows. We also had to cater for our son's university fees in the coming years.

These changes forced me to diversify and find a greater satisfaction in my career and life as a whole. If it was not for the crash, I would still be the employee I was before.

Now, I see myself as much more: as an author, video host, trainer, and opened to other options. People who have not met me in years comment that they do not recognize me. I am no longer the introvert that I was before. I have not become an extrovert, but have gained more self-confidence than I had before. The reading I have done and training I have followed have given me a different perception of myself.

CHAPTER 9

Reinvent Yourself

"History has demonstrated that the most notable winners usually encountered heart breaking obstacles before they triumphed. They won because they refused to become discouraged by their defeats." – B.C. Forbes

Jack Canfield often speaks about the task of reinventing yourself. The most difficult situations are when this skill is needed the most. Those are the times when you need to search out new information, expand your options, and apply even more diligence.

Personalysis©

My goal was to learn about people and their language of expectation. I wanted to do less convincing and more connecting to impact decision making. In a process called Personalysis©, this goal is a function of three areas: engagement, communication, and decision-making.

My success trail really started after spending 10 years in the insurance industry and after I joined my current company. Initially, I was recruited for my ability to change things. The people who interviewed me observed my red energy dimension. This means that once I have decided to do something, I am able to focus and act.

I am a certified trainer in Personalysis©, a tool which helps people discover their brilliance, do great work, lead full meaningful lives, and learn to thrive together in an ever-changing world. It demonstrates that all human beings share a common operating system, thinking patterns, feeling and behaviour that make up their personalities. But no two people are exactly alike. Everyone has a unique collection of characteristics, drives, and motivations.

Personalysis© offers you a way to better understand your personality and identify your dynamic pattern of strength and needs which may fluctuate. It offers insights about where and when you have the most and least energy, helping you use your gifts to thrive personally and professionally. The elements of Personalysis© consist of two primary elements: Dimensions and Colors.

The **Dimensions** represent your core needs for well-being. When these needs are met, you function well and thrive. The dimensions represent the kind of things you like to do, how you connect and communicate with others, and how you make decisions. Three dimensions exist: contribution, which is engagement, connection, which is communication, and commitment, which is decision-making.

The **Colors** represent your unique gifts: the tendencies, perspectives, needs, and strengths you have at different times. Red (expedite) is action continually moving forward with urgency. Yellow (collaborate) is adaptable, consulting before moving forward. Green (organize) focuses on detail, structure, and predictability. Blue (explore) anticipates the future, seeking clarity of trends and external information. Each one has a different profile. Once you identify the profile, the task is to work on the dimension based on your unique profile.

As I began my reinvention, I did not have enough money to invest into a business. Despite the financial crisis, I began to invest in myself. I investigated self-help books and found that I needed to build upon my training and operational expertise.

I wasn't a person who was into reading books. But I remembered hearing people say, "Readers are leaders." I started buying books almost every week and became a book-eater. I browsed the Internet. I started listening to prominent giants in the leadership genre. My Kindle collection consists of more than 200 eBooks. I read aloud to practice my pronunciation, diction, projection, and volume.

Financial Reinvention not Sacrifice

The lifestyle norms had changed for me as a Senior VP or Deputy CEO. Rather than thinking about my financial situation and need to invest as a sacrifice, I considered it as financial reinvention. The difference is a matter of leveraging my lifestyle norms from a prior time period to bolster my courage to make new priorities.

What came into my mind was, "What was I doing 10 years ago when I was making less than what I am making now? What was I doing?" I had no staff. I had no properties. I was living within my limited means. I thought, "Let me go back to that level of lifestyle and financial practice."

I had to financially reinvent. I had to sell properties to cover my financial exposure. I sold two properties to settle the mortgages. I gave up maid service and had to relinquish satellite television. I returned to washing my own dishes and cooking my meals at home. It was not the cultural norm for a Deputy CEO, but I was clearing the way to invest in myself.

It wasn't just financial. I cut my television time and converted it to reading time. I stopped my maid service and exercised by cleaning inside and outside the home. I was listening to audio books. I reorganized to save money despite the salary cut.

I remember reading a book that suggested that you become like water. If water has a broad space, it flows within that full space. If it only has a sliver of space, a crack, it will flow through that crack. I accepted the challenge and became like water. You must become like water and reinvent.

Change your priorities to focus on the essential necessities of your lifestyle. No more eating out every weekend. Prepare lunch instead of lunch trips during work hours. Whatever your extra expenditures, cut them.

When facing financial difficulties, many people do more of what makes them feel better. They will go out more and will distract themselves with fun and recreation. They increase their satellite television subscription because they are spending more time at home. But, the more sustainable opportunity is to invest in the activities that will build you.

Even now that the salaries have stabilized and increased, I am maintaining the same financial lifestyle. The extra savings are now going into an account for my son's education. I have added an exercise routine to my schedule. I continue to read and invest in books. I endeavor to read, learn, and share.

The Decision

In 2016, I made the decision, despite any financial strain, to reinvent myself and move into a new career after the company crashed. I decided not to make the mistake of counting solely on retirement with the company. As I normally do, I browsed Facebook.

I came across an advert from Jack Canfield offering an online trainer certification for the Success Principles. When I was in Botswana, I was looking for a similar course. At that time, I was close to enrolling in a John Maxwell course. I could not proceed due to the issue that occurred with the company and my return to Mauritius.

After sharing my vision with my wife, I enrolled for the certification using my savings. I considered this as an investment worth making. I opted for a pay plan and managed to complete the course within six months and become a Certified Trainer for the Success Principles. This was only the beginning.

In the environment I come from, people do not value online courses. I started visualizing attending a live course with Jack Canfield in the USA. A few weeks later, I received an email informing me of the Breakthrough to Success (BTS) workshop in Philadelphia scheduled for April 2017.

Lessons Learned

For your mind and body to work for you, you must understand your individual behaviors. You may not know how strong you are before a life crisis, but you need to have confidence in your ability to overcome situations that you find yourself in; the ability to bounce back from change and challenge. While what happens to us matters, it is actually how we react to what happens that demonstrates who we are. From Personalysis©, I discovered I have red energy, which has helped guide me in reinventing myself. While it is true that some people are born with some qualities that naturally move them forward despite setbacks, it is also true that you can develop resilience through an unrelenting, lesson-heeding approach to the experiences you go through in life.

Make it a conscious practice. Construct a vision for your future. Even when you are in difficult situations, you must reinvent.

Everyone needs purpose. I worked out my purpose as read, learn, and share. I sought certifications and found the Success Principles, certificates in understanding human behavior, Personalysis©, and *Happy for No Reason.*

These certifications enabled me to lead. I focused on me as a person, not as an employee. I didn't develop merely for the company. I developed myself focusing on moving ahead every day, doing new things.

You must work out your priorities. Many people will find excuses and complaints about their situation. They will find excuses to keep from doing things. Most of what I read suggested that this was no time to blame, make excuses, or complain. I had to review my financial plan.

CHAPTER 10

Seize the Opportunities

"Personal relationships are the fertile soil from which all advancement, all success, all achievement in real life grows." – Ben Stein

My Ghana Experience with Mr Brock

In the quest to live my life's purpose, I shared my dream with a friend who also used to be my CEO. He now lives and works in Ghana. He knew that I was conducting workshops on The Success Principles. In our discussion, we were looking for a way to penetrate the Ghanaian market and create awareness. During the discussion, he proposed that I speak in a conference being organized by his friend. Without any hesitation, I replied with a big yes.

This reminds me of the story about Microsoft founder Bill Gates. He proposed his initial operating system to IBM even though it wasn't ready for delivery. The conference topic was familiar to me so I felt ready to embark on this adventure. After several days, I was introduced to Alfred.

He was the conference organizer. After a brief discussion, I was accepted as speaker for the First Pan African Bancassurance Conference in Accra, Ghana. Prior to flying to Ghana, I went through my contact list to seize this opportunity to network.

This is when the work started. I began gathering loads of data to prepare for my talk. This task took me more than two months. Preparation is a vital key to success. From Brian Tracy to John Maxwell, books on presentation skills were on my desk night and day. All this to deliver only a 20-minute speech.

Finally, the day arrived. I boarded the flight to Ghana via Dubai. It was a long flight, but I was full of energy and eagerness. I connected with several people to expand my network and presented myself as a trainer in life assurance. My speech was entitled, "Embracing Disruption to Meet Customer Expectations from Protection to Enrichment".

Right after the Bancassurance Conference which was very beneficial for me as I managed to connect with more professionals, the AIO (African Insurance Organization) Conference was scheduled. I wasn't planning on attending that conference too, but I received an email from a CEO based in Accra, requesting a meeting at the conference. After my speech, I called the CEO to firm up our plans, but I got no answer. I attended the welcoming cocktail party, hoping to meet with him but did not see him. I asked some people around and was finally told that he did not attend the cocktail party. I met with other contacts and kept hope alive that I may meet with him the day after. I sent a WhatsApp message, but still no response.

The next morning, the day I was meant to catch my return flight to Mauritius, I was not sure what to do. Should I go to the conference venue and wait to be lucky? Or, should I stay at my hotel awaiting a message? My friend had to attend a seminar, so I decided to dress up professionally and accompany my friend. I would wait in the lobby. If I didn't catch the CEO, I planned to go back, freshen up, and make my way to the airport.

I waited for an hour and a half. I called the CEO, but still no response. I scanned every single person entering the lobby but could not find him. I had a few friends coming from my home country attending the seminar and met some of them. I was embarrassed when they asked me whether I was attending the conference. In fact, I told them I was waiting for someone with whom I had an appointment but didn't share my real issue.

The minutes ticked by and boredom set in. At some point, I decided to walk around. When I got back to the place I was initially sitting, I noticed it was already occupied by a tall guy in traditional attire. I kept watching him. I took the seat next to him. While sitting and observing, I noticed many locals greeting him. He was alone and I decided to start a conversation with him.

"You look very popular, Sir."

"Yes," he replied. "I am part of the organizing team and I'm waiting for my secretary," he continued. Immediately, I formulated a strategy connecting the words from our brief interaction. He introduced himself, saying, "I'm Mr. Brock."

I introduced myself and explained why I was there. We exchanged our business cards. After a brief exchange of other pleasantries, something in my mind—as if the angels were speaking to me—urged me to give him my profile. I opened my bag and handed him my last printed copy. He went through and I noticed his aura started to shine. He asked me several questions and wanted us to schedule a meeting to review his company profile.

He happened to be on the board of the insurance college. The college was in the process of setting up a training company. I said to myself, Wow! God is great. I've met the right person at the right time.

After our conversation, I was off to catch my flight. Just before embarking, I received an email from his secretary enquiring about my availability and interest in joining his team as a resource person. It was an opportunity to deliver training. Their company profile was attached. That was fast!

On my way home, I reviewed the profile with the help of a friend. Later, I was offered the opportunity to sit as a board member and buy shares of the company. Mr. Brock visited Mauritius with his father-in-law, Mr. Danku. We had a productive meeting, setting deliverables and planning.

Lucky or Prepared

Some people might think I was lucky. The question I asked myself: Was I prepared to be lucky? Did I attract the opportunity? Was I ready and prepared? Of course, the answer is yes. I prepared to be lucky. When luck showed up, I was there waiting for it. I decided to attend the initial meeting despite it not being scheduled. I had brought my profile with me as a tool to best present myself.

Jim Rohn said it best: "Don't pursue success. Attract it to you." That is what I did. Being at the right place at the right time. When I ponder over my situation, I believe I attracted this situation a long time back. After my certification as a trainer, my friend Javed said to me, "Think big, invest in a high-quality profile. This will show that you are already successful, and you can be trusted professionally."

He was right.

Had I not invested in the profile, Mr. Brock would not have been impressed. Life will not wait for you and you should not wait for everything in the universe to align in your favor. Rather, you should position yourself to attract what you desire out of life. Always be prepared and equipped— what would have happened if I didn't have a copy of my profile on me?

How many books do you read per week? How many personal or professional development trainings do you attend in a month or within a period of three months? You say you do not have enough funds to buy books or attend live trainings? Did you know that you could download many personal development books free of charge? Did you know that you could watch many training videos on YouTube? Did you also know that you could attend free personal development and other niche-based trainings online and offline?

Many people are not aware of this. Now, you are. Opportunities abound for you to tap into and become a better-informed person. Several strategies for success exist that are tested and proven. I am a product of many of these strategies. I beseech you to seek and embrace them as you come across them. You will benefit. I did.

Removing the Clay

Jack Canfield, in one of his workshops, shared the story behind the golden Buddha and how it was covered with clay. His wife made a comment that we are all golden Buddhas. Time, environment, education, and other factors cover us with clay and stop our glow. We may not remember that we are golden underneath.

With time, we lose confidence. Instead of feeling proud of being made of gold, we only see the clay. Our subconscious mind starts to accept that we have no value and are only made of clay— fragile, and without value.

The same idea applied to me. Because I was born into a poor family and bullied, I started to grow layers and layers of clay around me. The more the layer of clay grows the lower self-confidence drops. You lose the ability to see your options, vision, and direction.

Many people find themselves covered in clay. They have sight, but no vision. They live a sedentary life with no momentum. They are well-educated, have good marriages, and great kids. But they lack creativity, partnership, and legacy. They give their kids the best education, plan for retirement, look forward to grandchildren, and then wait for death.

These people had dreams when they were kids. They had visions of what they wanted to be as they grew up watching their roles models and movies. They had it all mapped out. With the enabling environment in place, they could have easily achieved their vision.

But with time, the clay covers them layer by layer, making them unattractive and uninspired. Their subconscious minds accept this false reality of life like a mirage in the desert.

I was no exception to being covered up with clay. However, I made the decision to take charge of my life. I had a new environment and I had a choice. Either I would continue my current journey cultivating the clay or I would make a U-turn and start on a new adventure.

If you really are not happy where you are, you only have two choices: stay where you are or work your way out of it. The former doesn't require any work. You only need to continue doing the things that you did before. You will continue to see the same results. However, if you want to begin to see things happen differently for you, you need to start *doing* things differently.

If you don't like your harvest, then you must change your seed. This is because the old seed will continue to give you the same old harvest. But when you change your seed, you are entitled to different harvests. In addition to this, if you want to create a new life and a new beginning for yourself, you must learn new habits and create new pathways.

You must also come up with new thought patterns. We are largely products of our thoughts, so you should be mindful and careful of the things that you allow to happen as well as the thoughts that you allow to take root in your mind. It was a decision I had to make as Tony Robbins always says, "Decide, Commit and Succeed." I made the decision, and as being beautifully explained by Jack Canfield, the word 'decision' is a derivative of the word 'decisive' which means 'to cut off.' So, I cut off the layers of clay and took control of my life. I started polishing the gold to make it shine again.

Lessons Learned

My greatest lesson here was to become resilient. Resilience is the ability to bounce back and bounce forward from bad circumstances that would have ordinarily swallowed you up.

In all my struggles and experiences, I was tempted to give up. Not once. Not twice. I was tempted multiple times, but I did not give up. I stuck to my guns. I knew that there was a better life out there. I had seen people live it. I knew I could have it, too. The most powerful young leaders are those who rise to a challenge and face it with courage. They possess an ability to inspire others to follow them and do things that they ordinarily could not do.

That is exactly what I did. You can do it, too. You have it in you to be all that you desire to be.

Many people believe that some can recover from unfavorable situations while others cannot. They believe that the problems they face and the situations that they find themselves in are too dire. I believe differently.

I am convinced that you can learn to be resilient, and your ability to bounce back from difficult conditions is not based on your genes or your life experiences: it's all up to you and your actions.

It was difficult to get rid of the old habits and thoughts. Every time I decided to change lanes, I was held back by memories of the past, personal problems, life challenges, and other barriers. I allowed myself to get clouded with low self-esteem, a sense of inferiority, and other self-imposed limitations.

Every time I had an opportunity, I shared my negative experiences and complaints with people. It is good to share your stories as a way of releasing your pain. I did it to my detriment.

Oblivious to me, by sharing my experiences, I was reassuring my subconscious mind that I did not want to come out from that situation. I was like two magnets that were inversely put together, pushing both sides apart. This situation lasted for years until one day my wife told me that I needed to let go of my past. She told me to use my experiences positively. That change made me stronger and courageous enough to make bold decisions.

Believe me, it is not that easy to let go, but you must. A technique I used was first to visualize the situation in color. Then turn the image to black and white. Slowly envision the image becoming smaller and smaller.

Finally, lock it in a box and throw the key into a running river. The small box remains in your mind, but the key is gone. You tell your subconscious mind that you cannot open the box again. Your mind focuses on other things. The box will remind you of the situation, but the images will be locked inside. Remember, our mind remembers images. Having done this exercise, I started removing the clay, layer by layer.

CHAPTER 11

Decide What You Want - Forget the How

"The indispensable first step to getting the things you want out of life is this: decide what you want." – Ben Stein

Often when we want to set a goal, we think about it. Then, we think about how we are going to achieve it. Many do not stick to the goal because they feel that they don't have the right tools: the capacity, the money, or the friends.

Like starting a new career with the Jack Canfield training, I had to reject the hesitation that came from not being able to afford it, not having any additional supports and not having any certainty in my job. I went ahead, knowing that my financial situation was precarious. And it worked out because I discovered that my life's purpose was to be a trainer and to train others. You cannot be a trainer without any references—no one to vouch for your ability and impact. You must be trained to do what you want.

I wanted to write and inspire. I wanted to write this book. I am not a writer, but I started with the outline and the first chapter. I looked for people who could help me.

The principle that titles this chapter could be applied to any environment from entrepreneurship to working with the elderly. I still had that self-restriction that sought to identify the barriers and stress over them. But I was able to let that inclination go with two simple steps. Decide what I want. Forget the how.

Developing the Speaker

The fire in my belly desired to move away from the financial and insurance sector. The company's lost reputation had affected all the employees working there. Some people blamed the personnel as the cause of the company's crash. Subsequently, both the company and I earned a bad reputation.

My aspiration was to do something else. I wanted a new job for the next 20 years and create a second career. My first idea was to go for something completely new. I browsed Facebook, not relying on my Plan A. But I quickly realized that I could not create something completely new.

I learned from Jack Canfield, "The shortest route is to read the one book with the 40 years of experience." Plan B was to utilize my experience in insurance for a professional development business for myself. I needed training.

The online training was the quickest and easiest way to get certified. I completed the online course and began to think about the fact that many online training options were available. Receiving certification online may be undervalued. After the online training, onsite classroom training was a must.

I decided to go to the in-person training. An email explained an opportunity in the United States for an in-person certification. But barriers flooded my thoughts. My salary was reduced to half. I reworked my financial plan, but I didn't have enough money for a trip to the United States.

I was determined to attend by any means. There was a payment plan for the conference fees. It was an agreement to pay over six months plus a service fee. I consulted my budget, and that cost spread over six months was doable.

I used my savings to pay for my flight. I knew it was a risk to do this—it was all the money that I had. What would I do if I went to the conference and learned nothing? How would I support my family? But I remembered what I learned in the online course. Don't get ahead of yourself. Don't worry about all the steps. Visualize your success and take the journey one step at a time.

The next task was to book the hotel. The air ticket and the conference fee left me without any money. I didn't fret. I said to myself, Fine. I will book for the conference and worry about the travel and the hotel later.

It was a couple of weeks later when the company I am working hosted its annual dinner. The minister in charge of the financial sector attended the dinner party. Politicians need to make popular decisions so that people will consider them wise and generous. The minister stood and announced that each employee would receive a one-month bonus. I was floored and almost in tears. The Success Principles immediately came to my mind. I had received the money for my hotel fees.

When you are building a house, you don't buy the furniture and the wallpaper along with the wood and the cement. You build the foundation first. You build systematically even though you don't have all the materials on hand initially. All you need is the vision of the result. You visualize the moment you are sitting and living in your house.

You visualize the lighting, the environment, the feeling. You take the next step and follow through. Through this, you are attracting everything that makes it possible for you to reach your goals.

Transformation of Me: Training Sessions

I traveled to Philadelphia to attend the training and enhanced my certification live with Jack Canfield. It was a 5 day fantastic experience listening to Jack and also involved with the practical exercises with other trainers around the world. Really a Breakthrough for Success. Back home I started to work on my plan. My friend Javed, a professional in PR directed me to invest in high quality profile with professional pictures which I did. The next logical step was to deliver training. I thought about setting a date for people to pay for the training. Brian Tracy Six Figure Speaker suggests that you answer a few questions before hosting your first training: Why will they come? What you will say? What will you share with them?

I asked myself, *Who am I as a trainer? What recommends me to audiences?* I decided that I would give potential clients something for free. Once they see the value in what I offer for free, people will hire me. I decided to focus on the audience that was already accessible: teams within my company. I customized the content of my presentation to the needs of insurance teams.

I presented the idea to a Sales Manager who always invites motivational speakers to boost the morale of his employees. He was happy to book a free training with such prestigious certification.

I posted the training experiences on my website. People were congratulatory. I conducted ten free trainings to promote myself. I was so prolific that online friends began to enquire whether I had changed jobs. All was going well. I printed materials at my own cost, but it was worth it because I was investing in my career and passion.

This new path was completely contradictory to the person that I thought I was. I was the one who spoke too softly in meetings, who was scared and nervous. But now, I was improving with every training. At first, I was an aggressive trainer. As I kept working, I learned to better manage the group process. Even when people said things to disturb, things that were unrelated to the presentation, I responded with calm and gentleness.

I worked out a feedback form and collected it at the end of each session. Some people will never say good things. If you are going into the woods, you will encounter mosquitoes. Some suggested more breaks, a better venue, food and snacks, and more. For a free training, I did not welcome these suggestions.

These are the mosquitoes. I began to lead with those considerations in my introduction. I took all the positive and constructive things to help me develop. Initially, I was annoyed by mosquitoes, but once I decided to work on myself, my frustration dissipated. I improved based on the feedback that I could afford to address.

Reading attracted my better angels. I found positivity and better relationships. If you want to buy a brand new Porsche, you will see Porsches everywhere. Similarly, when I transformed myself, I noticed many more people doing the same things. You attract people who are doing the same things. You can attract people who have the same mindset and energy as you. Because of this, I connected with a new network of friends.

I was saying "yes" instead of hesitating. My confidence was increasing. This was as in direct relationship to the experiences that I secured for myself. Before, I did not think public speaking was my cup of tea and had difficulty even saying my name. I felt stressed out just asking for items in shops. Now when I stand to speak, the fear that was present has vanished.

It became a family affair. As I continued to exhibit calmness, focus, and resolve, my wife began to read motivational books and engage with leaders. We began talking the same language. My network expanded across the world. My son began listening and conversing on motivational and public speaking topics at age 18. He doesn't say it explicitly, but I can see through his behavior and in the discussions that he has with others that he is picking up the lingo and the vibes in our home.

Releasing My Brakes

I realized after the free sessions and the experiences, networks, and family influence, that this Sorens was me all along. It may not have been my fault when I was young, but it is my responsibility now. By focusing on limitations, I was holding the brakes. I needed to release those brakes. But how?

My next task was to write a book. My thoughts betrayed me once again. I worried about who would be interested in my story. Why would someone choose my book over others? I did not know about the structure, how to put things together, how to outline.

I leaned on my prior experience and some intentional support from my network. Yes, there will be people who have a similar story. But, have they used their story and reached those who will respond? We think some people have a good background or a better coach. We believe we can't afford what they can afford. We second-guess ourselves because we are not one of these famous leaders.

I remembered the often-told story by motivational speakers of a man who walked on the beach every day at 6 in the morning. One day, he watched a man throw starfish into the sea. Other starfish continued to wash up on the shore.

"What are you doing?" the watcher asked.

"I must throw them in to save them."

"This is nature. Millions of starfish die each day. Your efforts won't make a difference for them."

The man picked up starfish and turned to the watcher as he threw it into the ocean. "This will make the difference. At least I have saved one."

It's not about changing the lives of millions of people. It is not about worrying about those you are not reaching. It is about changing life for those that you can reach. First, you must work out your life's purpose. You may want to share with many, but I urge you to just begin and don't stress over the numbers.

I decided to take a logical first step. I created the cover of my book. This was my "Act as If." I visualized my book and completed the cover. I included content about myself, and visualize what famous people would say about my book such as:

"One of the best books to lift you up"
"It will change your life"

I began to read online and from books about how to write and what to write. When you don't know, just Google. It's a sound piece of advice that I followed to my benefit. I worked on the first chapter and the second. The next chapters and the help came after. You are reading the results.

Lessons Learned

Every time I started my workshop, I used an example. You always need to have your plan. If you are planning to travel and you are new to it, you need to know your destination.

If you go to your travel agent and say that you wish to travel, they will ask you where you want to go. If you don't know where you want to go, they will not be able to tell you the cost, the clothing required, whether you need a visa, or any other steps you need to get to that destination.

You must make decisions with conviction, and things take shape. Believe in your dream and bring that belief to your decision-making. It will happen. Many people give up on the dream because they don't have everything they need. Just have the first thing. The rest will follow. Money, surroundings, family, friends should not be the stopper. Discipline yourself and do the five things that you need to do every day.

I wanted to start different businesses. People told me, "You will not make it. Be careful. I think you are crazy. We have just had a 55% salary cut. Do you think that's right?" I chose to listen to others who supported the idea.

I have changed from pessimistic to optimistic. I have moved from living in pursuit to beginning each day with meditation. I changed from not reading to reading voraciously. From night owl to early bird. I have grown beyond resisting for safety to going with the flow. I now move faster as I release the brake.

You will encounter critics, but all criticism is feedback. "Everything you want lies just outside your comfort zone. – Robert G Allen". With time, I have noticed that you will face issues outside your comfort zone. But if you move forward, you will bypass that critique and find your happiness.

How could I use my 25 years of experience to develop my plan? I blended my experience with the Success Principles. I started working with sales teams applying the Success Principles into my area of expertise. This helped me develop a reputation by leveraging my years of experience and adding the Success Principles.

Now, I can go into different fields, relating the Success Principles to multiple environments. I can work with finance, insurance, brick layers, and any others. The toolset can adapt to any sector.

Walking the Talk

For those which were not for its coming forth,
I said to them, Offend you I am loath,
Yet, since your brethren pleased with it be,
Forbear to judge till you do further see.
If that thou wilt not read, let it alone;
Some love the meat, some love to pick a bone.
-The Pilgrim's Progress

CHAPTER 12

Get the Right People Around You

"You're the average of the five people you spend most of your time with." —Jim Rohn

Your 5 People

The five people don't have to be physical. They can be experiences, understandings, or sources of information. The bad news is that you are impacted by those influences whether you like it or not. The good news is that you can control who you spend time with. My five people are competent information, self-talk, visualization, goals, and feedback.

Competent Information is delivered through books and doesn't need much explanation. You may read books about war, politics, business, or economics. You can choose autobiography or self-help. The topics that you ingest through reading influence and ideate who you are. It is that simple.

In this virtual-reality, social media, ever-changing, hyper-stimulated world, what you see affects your behavior.

Before I began my transformation, I was only reading what I had to read. I was only doing what was required. I was not intentionally expanding my self-development. Some people limit themselves. Some don't feel that they have the funds. Some don't invest in themselves. They don't realize the treasure of buying and reading a book.

If someone is successful, it is not only about money. It is also about knowledge. You may be looking to excel in training, sports, or some other passion. Be clear in your mind and know where you are going.

Knowledge + Skills + Massive Action = Change

If action is not taken, nothing happens. Knowledge can come through reading, watching videos, or from talking with knowledgeable people. Find the secrets and the success factors. You must learn how others have done it. For example, you can read about the invention of the light bulb. You don't have to go through all the trials Edison experienced. You can build on what he has accomplished. Now, we have neon lights, LED, and other options built on the original idea. It is the same with what you want from life. The books are lying on the bookshelf. The experience is found within them and you can build on them.

Helpful and Supportive Self-Talk is my second person. If you are thinking about problems, despair, and complaints, you will develop a bleak mindset. You will draw those experiences toward you. Continuous Negative News, or the CNN of your mind, must be turned off. When you turn off this drain on your creative energy, your conscious experience of the world and others will be different.

When you surround yourself with positive people, you become more positive. My perspective, routine, expectations are different because of the people in my social circle. Exercising the positivity muscle of my brain has brought about a holistic change. Who I am now is a result of the positivity I have attracted to myself.

How you speak to people and address solutions, plan your life and work all come from your thoughts. Change your thoughts and you will change the language with which you interact with the world.

**"Always start when it is finished. See the finished product
and then you will move forward." —Jim Rohn**

Meditative Visualization is my third person. Before you experience things physically, you experience them in your mind. The challenge is to keep the right images before you.

I have a routine to visualize myself in front of large crowds, sharing the Success Principles and the things I have learned. I close my eyes and see myself in front of 5000 people patiently waiting for me to start.

I work backwards as I open my eyes. How do I get 5000 people interested in what I have to say? It can be 100 sessions of 50 people. It can begin with 500 trainings of 10 people each. Start with those 10 people.

A leader recognizes that what they are absorbing, consciously and unconsciously, may manifest later. It is the continuity between one's vision and one's practice that maintains the certainty of the desired outcome.

Do not let go until you have manifested your dream. Each component of your body works in concert with your thoughts. You become what you think you are.

Clearly Stated Goals is my fourth person. Do you game plan? Do you have a written agenda? If you don't, you need to get one.

Recently, my son forced me to join the gym. Monday, Tuesday, and Friday, we worked out together. I was sleeping only four hours each night and had to wake up at 4:30 after only the few hours of sleep. I pushed through exhaustion because I knew that I had a task to accomplish.

I knew that I would reap the results of this temporary discomfort. I am aware that it is temporary because I have a plan. Plans are not just about starting but can encourage you to endure. If you knew you only had two years to attain your immeasurable success, you most likely would not spend those two years complaining. Instead you would get prepared, read the manual for maintenance, and start rejoicing.

Constructed Feedback is my fifth person. I call it constructed instead of constructive because all feedback can be reframed or constructed to benefit your ongoing development. People often stop working toward their goals because they fear what others might say.

Your coach, mentor, and your friends should motivate and encourage you to continue forward. They should encourage you to complete the first step. The next step will follow. They help you to explore the setbacks and create new opportunities out of your learning experience.

Mentors

Mentors provide value because they have been where you want to go. They also commit to giving you a portion of their time to help you along or to provide you with a sounding board or corrective guide. Connecting with a mentor is a skill.

Share what you want to do. Check to see that the person understands the vision that you see for yourself. He or she needs to have some experience in what you are doing. My mentor would be someone who has gone through some training experiences. He or she should know what it feels like to be in front of and engage with audiences. I want my mentor to be someone who has gone through successes and failures and knows how to respond to both.

The person must accept the role of mentor in your life. Look for people who can prepare you for the choices that you may face along your journey. The commitment they make to you connects with the commitment you are making to them. If you are not committed to put in the time and they aren't either, the project will never launch.

The mentors must agree to offer you the benefits of their expertise and give you feedback. They will need to ask you questions. Answer these questions honestly. You have to make an agreement with them about what you seek from this relationship. The agreement reminds you that the point is not to put you down or to make you feel bad. If there is a moment when they say something that you don't like, the agreement is critical to solving that conflict. The best mentors are going to care about your feelings but will also give information, guidance, and correct you.

Types of Mentors

There are some mentors who will push you to your limits with a military style. They are meant to challenge your ego and undermine your unfounded confidence, hoping to build you up after removing your negative aspects.

This mentoring style has its place. It can sometimes feel like humiliation, but it is usually offered in a safe space and a context that inspires. A useful analogy is that of sports. Challenging workouts and drills prepare your body and allow you to break through your physical limits.

When you are working toward your life's purpose, I believe that a better style of mentor is an encourager. They provide a continuous reminder of your 'why'. They affirm your purpose for what you are doing. You make the decision about the type of mentor you need. You may need both. In fact, it is advisable to have multiple mentors in your life.

CHAPTER 13

Give and Accept Feedback

"We have an innate desire to endlessly learn, grow, and develop. We want to become more than what we already are. Once we yield to this inclination for continuous and never-ending improvement, we lead a life on endless accomplishments and satisfaction." – Chuck Gallozzi

In my early years, feedback was criticism without construction. For me, it was humiliating. I was a punching-bag for those around me. I was often the butt of jokes.

People seemed to have fun bullying me. I became nervous, angry, and reserved. I was always in a defensive mood, susceptible to anger and reactive. I considered feedback as negative and did not accept people's criticism in a healthy way. The clay was building up on me. I was attempting to protect myself. I felt like people didn't want me to succeed.

Maybe you have experienced this too. Your critics might seem to be out to get at you. It may be that you are not well regarded, or that you feel like the victim. Everything people say can be taken as negative.

Many people react this way to criticism. A dog that has been hurt will always expect pats on the head to be painful. I urge you to fight against this presumption.

When I was in the midst of this, I thought to myself "I will someday be someone that they will respect." I did not realize it then, but I was utilizing the feedback, in my own small way.

I soon moved out of that environment. I connected with people who were more positive, supportive, and engaging. I was interested in changing my environment because the feedback I was receiving was negative and uncomfortable. The day I started my journey to self-development, I began to accept criticism as constructive.

If you are having a challenging time, change your environment. The books you read, television programs you watch, places you go—all these are filters for feedback. They influence who you are and how you behave. Choose activities and entertainment that are positive, progressive, and happy. You cannot blame the environment without action. Change your environment if you want to be different. Take that responsibility on yourself.

This reminds me of a commonly told story. Two persons were in a hole. One sits brooding over their doom. The other contemplating how they could get out. The first person continued to sit. The other began to dig in the hole to construct steps. He kept himself busy. His mind was occupied and his body was moving.

I realized that even though I was in a negative environment, I defaulted to acting like the person who began to create steps. I sought to change my environment.

Receiving Feedback

Whenever someone offers you feedback, be sure to listen so that you can use the information to your advantage. It is a map that will show you whether you are on course or off course. Take it to test yourself. Are you moving toward your goal or sliding away from your objective? I agree that it is not easy, but you must get used to it. Another author I respect is Spencer Johnson, who suggests that feedback is the breakfast of champions. Let people tell you how you are moving forward.

This is what I call CPD = Continuous Personal Development. I have often read feedback comments, such as "it was confusing," "too long," "too short," or others that did not fit in a constructive criticism model. At first, I refused feedback for this reason. I considered my initial training as free of charge. They don't get to review my work without paying for it.

But they are paying something. They are giving their time. They are responding to the needs they identify. When they respond, they are working *for* you, not *against* you. Even when they give feedback that is hurtful, they are offering you an opportunity to be better. For example, a respondent may say, "I think it would be better with a better trainer."

They are communicating that they did not get what they wanted. The needs of your audience are changing every day. The question is, how can you become that better trainer? Is it a matter of bringing new information to the training? Does it imply setting up their expectations beforehand? Remember, when you are in the forest, you will get mosquitoes. You get to choose whether to hold on to feedback or let it go. You are not required to accept all feedback. Your focus is to achieve your developmental goals.

Giving Feedback

My experience with giving feedback is to offer advice that will help people move forward. I enrolled in an online training course. I was not completely happy with the course. Rather than complaining, I provided feedback to the professionals developing the course. I continued with constructive feedback. One day I was contacted by the developer, who offered me a 25% discount if I would agree to continue providing her with the feedback.

When you are part of someone's success, it increases your happiness, too. If you request help or a service, you receive a level of service that the helper is capable of giving. That person engages with a level of service that fulfills their purpose. It is deeper than the amount they receive in payment. When you provide feedback and exchange interactively, you participate in a relationship that brings happiness. I always tell people to be happy for no reason. You will soon develop a reason to be happy.

Ego

When I was learning business, I came across a case study about Blackberry. They were innovative in their approach and was once the biggest smartphone maker. They failed to innovate according to customer needs. They were so successful that they refused to innovate using the feedback that was coming to them.

What happened? Blackberry is no longer the leader in the cell phone business. Apple, Samsung, and other brands have included the features that Blackberry had and expanded upon them. Their refusal to act on the feedback crippled their innovative edge in the market and eventually cost them market share. [4]

Provide whatever your work is to the market consumers who will make use of your work. They are the users that will give you feedback. You must listen. You may emphasize that you know what you want and what you intend. You may think that you want to continue the course without the feedback. But, if you don't, you will not improve.

Putting aside ego, I changed the slides of my training presentation each time I delivered it. Satisfying customer needs is the key for success. If you want to be successful in whatever you do, you must have the ability to change, be flexible, adaptive and always re-strategize. I was learning whether the presentation was attractive or not. Had I not done this, I would have missed opportunities to improve.

---

[4] Tom Taulli – Lessons From The Fall Of Blackberry September 2013

CHAPTER 14

Prepare for Success

"The secret of getting ahead is getting started. The secret of getting started is breaking your complex, overwhelming tasks into small manageable tasks, and then starting on the first one." – Mark Twain

Anyone aiming to be successful needs to have faith that motivates action. As Les Brown rightly put it, "Feed your faith and your doubts will starve to death!" Success is a trail with lots of ups and downs and you must be prepared for everything.

Being Prepared

My meeting with Mr. Brock in Ghana was not a stroke of luck, even though many of my friends still believe it was. It was a case of preparedness meeting opportunity which resulted in the successes and business deals I struck with Mr. Brock's organization. That singular event further prompted me to believe that anything is possible.

You need to be sensitive and act according to your instinct and intuition. I could have stayed back at my hotel room that day, lazing away until I left for the airport.

But I didn't do that, I decided to try once more to see if I could find the CEO. When my efforts were in vain, I did not let that dampen my spirit. I remained cheerful, greeted people whom I saw at the conference and was alert enough to notice people greeting Mr. Brock. I introduced myself to him and the rest, as they say, is history.

Preparation is a mix of gaining competence and acting intentionally. You only see the ease of the duck gliding upon the water. You don't see its feet paddling frantically below. Likewise, when you demonstrate your expertise, your preparation will make it look effortless. But you will have put in the time to get ready prior to the experience.

People only see your success, but behind that success is a lot of effort. The motivational speaking training experience was part of my effort. I was thinking about what I was already doing: training for sales. It was in line with my mantra to Read, Learn, Share. It was a natural progression to start there.

Initially, I was thinking big. Find a venue! Fill it up! Be successful! But the question that grounded me, "Why would someone attend my training?" Your confidence increases when you develop the answer to "Why will they listen to me?" After the first couple of training sessions I gave, I was gratified by the responses and the ability to practice.

Similar training was presented over many years by Jack Canfield. Human beings need repetition to change their unconscious minds toward new habits. You must continue telling them to take responsibilities, decide what is desired, believe it is possible, attract the good things, set your goals, take small steps, learn from successful people, and create confidence.

Release the brakes and tell yourself that it can be done. See what you want in the future and act as you would if you have achieved all you want. If you don't act, your goal will not be completed. Now, I have done it. I know that people will come to my training. They know what they need.

Social Media

After reaching a crowd I was familiar with, I had the firm intention to create the desire to learn and awareness of the Success Principles. My target market was to move into Africa. I wanted to be the Jack Canfield of Africa. I wanted to share it with people that really needed the principles to be successful. My target was to help the people around me.

On Facebook, I posted content and tagged some friends of mine. I also boosted the viewing based on a target population by age. This is the strategy. If you want an apple, you can't just wish for it. You will need to plant the seed. I set a budget for boosting the campaign to get the word out. People that I didn't know quickly started to respond and like my videos. It was slightly embarrassing at first, to see myself in videos online, but I soon got used to it.

I posted pictures on my Facebook page and showcased my training. My friend in Botswana invited me to come and give a presentation to his group. It would have been difficult for me to make the participants aware without the use of Internet. Social media allowed me to bridge this distance.

I was selected to attend a workshop in Johannesburg by the company. I decided to extend my stay and fly to Botswana on my own cost, to deliver a presentation there. Fifty plus graduates registered for my training in Botswana. They became ambassadors for my brand.

This inspired me to think about writing my book. Some people will read the book and not be satisfied. But I want to share my experience. The only thing you need is the right people. You need to get the procedure and get started. My trainer experience was a stepping stone to the book. You must create new habits outside your comfort zone.

Awareness and Exposure

I am now preparing and uploading YouTube videos about every two weeks to remind my followers about the principles that I discuss. It also serves to introduce different principles. Subscribers can learn about all the Success Principles and gain some breadth of information. If people want more, I am open to scheduling paid training sessions.

I send proposals out. I created the reference points through the online videos, social media, and word-of-mouth from participants in my previous sessions. We are using all the avenues to create and sustain awareness. Recipients of my proposals can browse online and view what I have done

How do I market to people? I create video clips that become small trailers as shown during a movie. They become a collage of training videos, pictures, materials and more. You visualize the picture of the various components of a house. You decide upon the number of floors. You then move to the foundation. This is what I did. I began with a foundation for free.

My confidence increased. Whenever you have something you want to achieve, do it even if you are not being paid. When you are not well-known, you need to invest by doing things. This takes time. Failure will happen. Jack Canfield had to face 144 rejections. He was accepted the 145th time. One day, it has to click. All successful people started with small steps, from point A to point B.

Many spend too much time worrying about their marketing and name recognition. They wonder if they are credible, popular, or educated enough to do what their heart desires. My message is similar to what Tony Robbins' said: "Get the knowledge and skills, but those are nothing without massive action." You must do everything that is in your power to do today. Don't worry about tomorrow and the tasks of that day. Act today.

I'm working on another training in Ghana. The important factor that influenced the decision makers was the experiences I have and the marketing I undertook on social media. The next steps will come naturally. The more you learn, the more confident you will be. This can be translated into other areas. When I received a proposal to talk in Ghana, I believed that the deciding factor for my selection was my experience. They don't know whether I was paid or not for the experience. They only know that I have presented, and that it was successful.

CHAPTER 15

Do It Afraid

"You have to believe in yourself when no one else does.
That's what makes you a winner." - Venus Williams

I am much more confident now, but I understand fear. I was there for a good portion of my life. How do I start? Where do I start? People don't have a point of reference that supports my expertise or credibility. In addition to wrestling with those thoughts, I had to get over the stress of public speaking.

We worry about everything. It doesn't make sense to worry over things that you can't control or things that are beyond the next choice you make. Only focus on the next step. Your next approach is to come to terms with the fear that rises within you masquerading as caution. Often, you must stand up and do things while you are still afraid. If you wait until the fear dissipates, the moment has passed.

Thinking Big

My friend who helped me with PR told me to think big. I sent emails to a few people. Three people responded positively to the advert. Do I go ahead with 3 people, or do I postpone? I asked myself. Sleep with a problem, wake up with a solution. The thought occurred to me, I have over 500 salespeople working with me in the sales department. I proposed to one of the managers that I could share my training with the sales team in a workshop. The manager accepted.

I held a half-day training session with them. The manager began to talk about it. I went on, giving other sessions. The manager shared it with other regional sales managers and I was requested to deliver the training to their teams. At the end of July 2019, I had completed nine sessions with the sales team and one with my team. I also completed one session in Botswana.

You should not wait for the ideal situation to be in place before you start living your dreams or launch out to create an impact and bless humanity. If the ideal situation is in place, it is good, but if not, remember the words of a favorite coach of mine, John Obidi, "Do it afraid."

Begin to talk, act, and even dress as if you have reached the destination you are moving toward. Soon the Law of Attraction will kick in. The Law of Attraction, which I have personally experienced, draws people, resources, and opportunities toward you that are in line with and resonate with the energies that you put out.

This is why it is very important that as you read this book, start being mindful of the type of thoughts you allow to take root in your mind and the beliefs you hold in your heart. You need to start being intentional about the company you keep, the interactions you entertain, and the vibes you give off. These things go a long way to determine how you show forth and appear before people. It forms the perception that they consequently have of you.

You Can

I have heard many people say, "I can't do it!" They say it so convincingly. What I see in anyone who says this is a person who is unwilling to change.

I see a person who is afraid to take new steps. Such a person is satisfied with the norm. He is afraid to challenge the status quo and so prefers to remain in his comfort zone.

However, one thing I have come to learn is that no one can make a difference if he stays in his comfort zone. I have never seen anyone who made waves and noticeable impact describe the path as smooth and rosy. Often, they had to do things and go places that they ordinarily wouldn't dare. But they did it anyway and they are better for it. They "did it afraid" and faced their fear. They were able to see fear as what it is, all smoke and mirrors.

Attitude and Optimism

Attitude is everything. What is your attitude like? The act of turning a challenge into opportunity is not always as easy as it sounds. Your attitude matters because it determines what you put out and how you filter what comes to you.

When you are optimistic and confident, nothing is too difficult for you to achieve. You will scale heights and go beyond yourself to do great things. But if you are not, you will see only the potholes and obstacles on your path and give yourself reasons for not being able to achieve what you set out to.

Though not all of us are born optimists, it is a quality that can be learned. An optimistic learner is one who sees anything that happens to him as an opportunity to learn and grow.

Optimists have been found to do better academically, to perform better in athletics, and generally do better on all of their tasks.[5] They have better coping skills. They are less likely to succumb to sadness and depression and enjoy better overall physical health. The most reassuring part is that people can be taught how to be more resilient than they were before, by adopting lifestyles that will promote optimism and aid resilience.

One of such lifestyles is what I call a lifestyle of CPD – Continuing Personal Development. This means that whether it has to do with my personal life, my relationship with my family, friends, acquaintances, or professional life—the way I do my work, carry out duties assigned to

---

[5] Psychology of Sport and Exercise – Gordon Randall 2008

me, and relate with my colleagues, subordinates or superiors; I am always working on myself.

I am constantly reading books on self-improvement, studying people and how they behave, observing why they do the things they do, understanding the business of being social, what makes people tick, and more. I am doing this in addition to all the studying and training I do because I realize that people are the new currency.

There is no limit to what you can do if you keep a diverse network. It would also determine how far you will go in your business and life. Your network is your net worth. From time to time, as and when I need to, I tap these relationships to help me get over unfavorable situations, bounce forward, and be the best that I can be.

I am currently carrying out research even though I have no workshop booked. I'm doing things to get myself prepared and ready should I be offered a speaking or training opportunity. I am also preparing videos and audios and publishing them on my Facebook account with the aim of showcasing and publicizing my brand as a speaker and trainer.

I am doing this now to project myself into people's subconsciousness with the objective to get hired as a speaker. You never know who is watching, listening, and following you on social media. You don't know what opportunities may crop up at any time.

The relationship between possibility and action is like working out. You focus on the purpose and consistency. That's how you achieve the results. You don't achieve anything if you sit on the sidelines watching others and wishing about what you could do. You don't achieve if you only do it once without a commitment.

If you do push-ups once a year, you will not build any muscle. But if you so three sets of 12, three times per week, you'll build muscles. Get the right equipment. Prepare yourself and you'll be more likely to succeed. Set the scene and follow through. This is what I have been doing and will continue to do.

CHAPTER 16

Transform

"You must take personal responsibility. You cannot
change the circumstances, the seasons, or the wind, but
you can change yourself." – Jim Rohn

Being in Botswana, away from the group's crash when it happened, I
experienced it differently. It was God's plan. I did not witness the crash like
my colleagues. It reminds me of the story of the man who was scheduled to
work in one of the World Trade Center buildings on September 11th, 2001.

He went about his normal routine, rising early and on his way, to
work stopped by his favorite coffee shop. A mishap with the coffee lid
spilled hot coffee down the front of his shirt. More than the pain and the
unexpected incident of the hot coffee, he was annoyed that he would now
reach his office later than planned because he had to go back home and
change his shirt. It was a redirection that took him an hour both ways.
He would have reached his office building at 9:30 any other day. But he
was late, and missed it.

Because I was not in the middle of the chaos at my company headquarters, I experienced the challenges differently. Whereas some of my colleagues may have felt despair and the panic of being close to the center of the dramatic situation. I was far enough to reflect on my own mortality, my view of the world, my purpose, and my goals. I was spared from the worst of it, and that clarity within the salvation opened a worldview for me that took me back to the beginning; having my parents as my first role models.

They are, without a doubt, my role models. Those who never liked us also form part of my success. They helped me build a stronger character resulting from all their insults and gossips. Nothing in life is a mere coincidence. It is what you want to make out of your life that will impact your future. Your choices are what can bring you down or make your success skyrocket. After years of sacrifices, I started to build my house with the help of my beloved parents.

We cherished the good times, but we endured bad times as well. As a little kid, I was bullied a lot by my neighbors and cousins. My cousins were always belittling my family and myself for being poor. They said that we were tarnishing the family name as we were poor, and they were wealthy in monetary terms.

All this made me sad and depressed. I was not happy and I really wanted the bullying and hurtful comments to end. Can you imagine a child having to endure these comments? Once again, this phase of my life helped to carve my personality and made me stronger in a positive way.

In addition to this, my father's alcohol addiction only made my relatives' gossip and disrespect worse. Despite the gossips and hurting words, I never lost hope at my tender age and continued to believe. And I am confident that the art of believing at that time helped me to achieve my goals today.

The great Mahatma Gandhi said: "You can't change how people treat you or what they say about you. All you can do is change how you react to it." Gandhi was right.

I learned how to constructively react to the gossips from people and this really helped me. You reap what you sow. I sowed patience, perseverance and tolerance and today by Almighty's grace, I am reaping happiness and peace of mind.

I could have let what the people in my neighborhood were saying get to me, but I intentionally did not allow it. From a very young age, I identified with my family and even though we were not rich by any standards, we had one another and that was enough for me.

Appreciate the Now

Every time I left for work, my father saw me off. I was always telling him, deep within my heart, "Please wait for me." I felt close to my father, but could never express it to him. I had issues with neighbors and others. I didn't cultivate peace, or express my gratitude and appreciation to others. Just like a beaten dog does not allow you to pet him, I was acting in the same way. Everyone was busy doing things to make ends meet. It wasn't an environment where you could show affection.

I'm still like this. I wanted my father to wait for me whenever I returned. My mom always used to wait for me. In 2015 when I came back from Botswana, it was different. The lights were off. I guessed early the next morning I would meet my mom. The next morning, my brother came to tell me that dad was not well. I went with him to see my father.

When I arrived, my father's eyes lit up with joy. I sat next to him and gave him a sip of water. He was having trouble breathing. He leaned on my shoulder as I sat next to him. He passed away on my shoulder. Everyone told me, "He was waiting for you." I felt a close bond with him, but I could not express it. We connected silently, and he had heard my wish. Even in that sad moment, I was happy that he had waited for me before departing.

The lesson for me relates to love. When you love someone, tell them. Don't wait. Appreciate what you have before you regret what you had. I want to recommend that you share your love, gratitude, and appreciation freely.

The universe will listen to you and provide the path for you to receive what you want. It was silent from my heart, but it was powerful for me. Some people complain in a difficult situation. You are attracting negativity with that energy. Change that energy to positive and attract positive things.

Oprah was addressing a college graduation. She presented three personal directives to ponder:

Know who you are. You need to describe who you are and where you want to go.

Always be of service. Be kind. At least, in your interactions, create a sense of peace.

Always do the right thing. Determine who your actions impact, what the influence is, and how you can improve upon it.

When you leave this world, your body returns to dust. We think death is like traveling on a plane. We take our bags and other things with us. When you sleep, you leave everything. Death is more like that. Work out your life purpose while you live so that the baggage you leave influences in the way you intend it to.

Principles

The principles I covered in this text have been won through a life of struggle and reinvention. They serve as a pattern for your opportunity to find your purpose amid loss, redirection, or struggle.

Role Models

People all over the world have overcome circumstances that should have crushed them down just because they kept a happy disposition. Just think of Oprah Winfrey—why do you think her show was on for more than twenty-two years? Because people love listening to how others overcome challenges, and triumph over hardships.

Think of a leader that you admire. It may be someone from your school or someone from history or popular culture. The most likely reason why you admire him or her maybe he or she has a compelling personal story about meeting a challenge and getting to the other side.

Let's have a look at some people who have impacted their worlds greatly and turned out successfully. They are the ones that faced the most challenges, but they overcame those challenges to become high-flyers.

Nelson Mandela, the noble South African, was the first in his family to attend school. He was imprisoned for his fight against the repressive apartheid regime that prevailed in South Africa from 1964 to 1990. He never compromised his position against apartheid. He spoke out against apartheid, was imprisoned, and released after 27 years, when agitation for his release reached an all-time high. In 1994, became the first democratically elected President of South Africa.

Oprah Winfrey famously tells the story of her very difficult and abusive childhood and poverty in rural Mississippi, which certainly didn't stop her from becoming the world's first black woman billionaire. She is undoubtedly one of the most influential woman in the world.

Sir Paul McCartney applied to join the choir of the Liverpool Cathedral and was turned down because they didn't think he was a good enough singer. As one of the Beatles, and then on his own, Paul McCartney became one of the most successful singers/songwriters of all time. McCartney was even bestowed with a knighthood. He is listed in the Guinness Book of World Records as the most successful musician and composer in popular music history.

Drew Barrymore, an actress, was abandoned by her father before she was born. Neglected by her mother, she became addicted to alcohol and drugs at just nine years old. Now as one of the most successful actresses of her generation, she has not only had longevity in acting (a career spanning more than 20 years) but has also become a successful film producer through her own company, Flower Films.

Albert Einstein's mother was told to take her son home and teach him by herself because the school could no longer cope with him. One of his teachers had said that he "would never be able to do anything that would make any sense in this life,"[6] but Einstein went on to publish more than 300 scientific works, and more than 150 non-scientific works, and received the 1921 Nobel Prize in Physics.

Vidal Sassoon came from a poor family in London and, when his mother could no longer care for him, spent six years in an orphanage. He didn't have access to the best salon jobs because of his cockney accent, so the now world-famous hairdresser who invented the bob haircut took three years of voice lessons and started his own salon. Sassoon went on to re-invent the world of haircutting and styling.

---

[6] Einstein a Life – Denis Brain

There are many more of these types of people that I have mentioned throughout the text. I challenge you to look at any other successful persons that you know. They will have a story describing how they overcame odds somewhere in their life path. My challenge to you is to engage your own achiever's trail.